WAKE
UP
AND
COOK

TRICYCLE BOOKS FROM RIVERHEAD

Wake Up and Cook:
Kitchen Buddhism in Words and Recipes
edited by Carole Tonkinson

Meeting the Buddha:
On Pilgrimage in Buddhist India
edited by Molly Emma Aitken

Big Sky Mind:
Buddhism and the Beat Generation
edited by Carole Tonkinson

WAKE UP AND COOK

Kitchen Buddhism in Words and Recipes

edited by

Carole Tonkinson

A Tricycle Book

Riverhead Books,

New York

Riverhead Books
Published by The Berkley Publishing Group
200 Madison Avenue
New York, New York 10016

Book design by Richard Oriolo
Cover design by Charles Woods
Cover photograph © by Joanne Schmaltz/Photonica

A continuation of credits appears in the acknowledgments on pp. 219–228.

First edition: January 1997

The Putnam Berkley World Wide Web site address is
http://www.berkley.com/berkley

Library of Congress Cataloging-in-Publication Data

Wake up and cook: kitchen Buddhism in words and recipes / edited by Carole
Tonkinson.—1st ed.
     p.   cm.
     "A tricycle book."
     ISBN 1-57322-575-4
     1. Food—Religious aspects—Buddhism.   2. Cookery—Religious aspects—
Buddhism.   3. Religious life—Buddhism.   4. Cookery, Oriental.
I. Tonkinson, Carole.
BQ4570.F6W35   1997
294.3'4446—dc20   96-22923
                                                                        CIP

Printed in the United States of America

10 9 8 7 6 5 4 3 2 1

"Once you know how
the dough becomes bread,
you will understand
enlightenment."
—Shunryu Suzuki Roshi

Contents

Introduction

A man traveling across a field encountered a large tiger. He fled,
the tiger after him. Coming to a precipice, he caught hold of the
root of a wild vine and swung himself down over the edge. The
tiger sniffed at him from above. Trembling, the man looked down
to where, far below, another tiger was waiting to eat him. Only
the vine sustained him.

Two mice, one white and one black, little by little started to
gnaw away the vine. The man saw a luscious strawberry near
him. Grasping the vine with one hand, he plucked the strawberry
with the other. How sweet it tasted!

—Paul Reps retelling a parable the Buddha told in a sutra

Tibetan Buddhist teacher Ane Pema Chodron describes
the condition of being on a cliff with tigers above and
tigers below as "the predicament that we are always in, in
terms of our birth and death." In this parable, she sees the
following teaching: "Each moment is just what it is. It might
be the only moment of our life, it might be the only strawberry
we'll ever eat. We could get depressed about it, or we could
finally appreciate it and delight in the preciousness of every

single moment of our life." It is in this spirit that this collection of food stories, meal blessings, and recipes are gathered: they are calls to wake up, when we cook and when we eat, when we stir a pot or pluck a ripened fruit.

In recognizing these ordinary, everyday activities as opportunities to awaken, we return to ancient teachings: from Buddha's own enlightenment, which was preceded by a meal, to the words of celebrated masters and contemporary cooks who bring the mind of enlightenment into monasteries, modern urban kitchens, meditation centers, and Zen bakeries and restaurants. What all these cooks and eaters have in common is an approach to food that encompasses Way-seeking mind.

A Zen cook, for example, cooks with an essential understanding that to harvest food and to eat is a celebration of the interconnection of all life and a recognition that these are holy endeavors—every bit as holy as sitting in a meditation hall or offering incense and alms at a temple. Zen master Dogen wrote of this practice: "Only those who have aroused this mind [Way-seeking mind] can know it, and only those who practice this mind can understand it. Therefore, you should look after water and grain with compassionate care, as though tending your own children." This collection offers the words and experiences of those who have followed this path with the intention that they might arouse the spiritual aspiration that can transform each moment of our lives—in the kitchen and out—into enlightenment.

These brief anecdotes, teachings, blessings, and recipes offer a rough road map for bringing a spiritual path into your own kitchen, whether you're a Buddhist or not, if you cook and if you don't. Read them simply as a set of instructions on how to cook a meal or as guidelines on how to cook your life; according to the Zen master Dogen, it amounts to the same thing.

All texts and recipes retain their original spelling, style, and usage. Unless otherwise noted in the acknowledgments, all recipes are courtesy of *Tricycle* editors.

Awake

Buddha *means* awake, *and to awaken—to be enlightened—is the aspiration of all who follow in the Buddha's footsteps. In order to find an answer to the pain and suffering of human life, the young Prince Siddhartha Gautama chose to leave his life of princely luxury and lead instead a stark, ascetic existence. For six years, he consumed the minimum amount of food necessary to survive— sometimes only a single grain of rice and one sesame seed each day. One day, after he fainted from hunger and was unable to continue in his meditation, the Buddha-to-be put an end to his self-mortification and embarked upon a new course, a path of moderation. His followers perceived Siddhartha's choice to live moderately—particularly his decision to eat food to sustain his practice—as a sign of weakness, but the young prince-priest held firm. It was not long after his fellow seekers deserted him that Siddhartha accepted an exquisite alms offering, a rich dish of rice milk, and it was this meal that nourished him in the days of sustained meditation that culminated in his awakening. This poetic retelling of the Buddha's abandonment of asceticism and embrace of moderation appears in a Burmese manuscript adapted and translated by Michael Edwardes.*

After a time, five priests passed through the jungle on their way for rice, and came where the prince-priest was. He had been there six years, and they received the impression that he was soon to become a Buddha. They therefore remained with him, sweeping the enclosure, cooking rice, and doing other things suitable to be done. The prince-priest, having arrived near the time of his change to a Buddha, attempted a very long fast and refused to eat even the least kernel of rice . . . Thus, by his extreme fasting, he became exceedingly faded, and his appearance, though formerly like the purest gold, was now black, and the thirty-two [physical] signs of Buddhadom disappeared. While thus fasting, and being overcome by his extreme hunger, he fell down in a most pitiable manner in the place where he was walking. . . .

After this he considered that abstinence was not the means by which he should become a Buddha, and he took his rice-pot and went forth again for food. When he had so done and had eaten, the thirty-two signs of his becoming a Buddha again appeared, and his appearance was again like gold. The five priests who were with him said, "He has been six years doing penance for the sake of becoming a Buddha, and he cannot attain that state; therefore he goes out again in search of food. If he continues to use the mixed food he obtains, when will he become a Buddha? He has left the jungle, and now goes about only with a view to becoming rich. As a person who wishes dew with which to wash his head, must look for it, so, if we cannot obtain Enlightenment in his presence we must go where we can get it. Of what profit is he to us?" Then they left him, took their rice-pots, and went into a jungle a hundred and forty-four miles distant.

In those days, in the jungle of Uruvela was a village called Senani; in that village was a rich man who had a daughter called Sujata. She had arrived at the state of puberty and was in the habit of praying at the foot of a certain Banyan tree, thus: "Verily, if I can obtain a husband who will be a suitable match for me, and by him a son, O god of the trees, I will each year offer you one hundred thousand." Her prayer was granted. On the full moon of May, after Gautama had been in the jungle six years, Sujata prepared her offering for the god. In the first place, she had a thousand cows fed in a place of sweet vines and their milk given to five hundred cows; then the milk of the five hundred was given to two hundred and fifty. In this manner she kept milking and feeding them, till she had reduced the number to eight. Thus this milk was some hundred times richer and sweeter than common milk. Sujata, wishing to make her offering early on the full moon of May, arose and milked her eight cows. The calves of the cows were not near them, nor had they drawn any of the milk; yet, as soon as she set her pot under the udders, the milk began to flow in streams. When she saw this extraordinary thing, she took the milk with her own hands, and put it into a new pot, and set it over a fire which she herself had kindled. The milk, while cooking, sent up large bubbles, and each, after turning three times to the right, sank again, and not a drop boiled over. Not the least particle of smoke arose from the fire. While the milk was boiling four kings came and watched it. The king of the gods came and kept up the fire. The gods put honey and other heavenly food into the pot. On this occasion, and on the day Gautama [the Buddha] entered Nirvana, the gods put their food in while the pot was boiling, on other occasions, after the food was cooked. Sujata discovering so many strange signs, called a female servant and, saying she had never seen so many signs before, directed her to go and clear a place under the tree where she would come with the offering.

On the day when a Buddha is created, it is customary for him to receive a golden cup worth one hundred thousand. On that account it was put into Sujata's mind that she should pour her preparation of milk into a golden cup; she therefore ordered another, worth one hundred thousand, to be brought. Then she took the pot and poured the milk into the golden cup, and as water slides from the leaf of the lily without leaving traces, so the milk glided from the pot to the golden cup and just filled it. She then put over it another golden cup, dressed herself in all her ornaments, placed the golden cup upon her head, and with elegant steps went to the Banyan tree. When she saw the priest, she supposed him to be the god of the trees, and approached curtseying, until she arrived near him. Then she took the cup from her head and placed it by him together with a pitcher of perfumed water. At this time the rice-pot given him by the Brahma disappeared, and he, looking about and seeing no rice-pot, reached out his right hand and received the perfumed water. She then placed the golden cups, with the boiled milk, upon his hand. Thus, having offered the golden cup with the same feelings with which she would have offered it had it been only a leaf-cup, she returned home.

The prince-priest arose from his place, and going three times to the right round the Banyan tree, took the cup and went to the bank of the river Neranjara, where there was a bath in which more than one hundred thousand Buddhas had bathed on the day of their receiving infinite wisdom. Having set down the cup, and bathed, he put on the robe which more than one hundred thousand Buddhas had worn before him, and remained with his face to the east. He then divided the milk into forty-nine equal parts, each about the size of the palm-fruit and, after, returned to the Banyan tree, and took no other food than one of these portions of boiled milk each day. On the forty-ninth day he became a Buddha. There he remained, without bathing or stretching, but passed the time in happiness. When he had eaten the last of the milk, he took the cup, and said, "If I am verily to become a Buddha today, let it go up the river; but if I am not, let it float down the stream." This said, he threw the cup into the river. The cup floated into the middle of the stream, and then went up the river for eighty cubits, with the velocity of a very swift horse. It was then engulfed in a whirlpool, went down to the country of Kala, a serpent-king, and making a noise by striking the three golden cups of the last three Buddhas it stopped under them. The serpent-king, hearing the noise of the cups striking together, said, "Yesterday there was one Buddha, today there is another," and in more than a hundred stanzas he repeated praises to the Buddha and arose from his sleeping place.

A Simple Rice Pudding

S e r v e s   4 – 6

Not *nearly as rich as the fragrant rice milk the Buddha consumed,
this rice pudding offers sustenance, nonetheless.*

⅓ cup short-grain white rice (such as Arborio),
     uncooked

½ cup sugar

4 cups milk

⅔ cup raisins (optional)

     Freshly grated nutmeg

3 tablespoons butter

½ cup heavy cream

Sprinkle the rice onto the bottom of a buttered casserole dish.
Stir sugar into the milk; add raisins, if desired. Pour the milk
mixture over the rice; sprinkle with a little grated nutmeg and
dot with butter. Place in a (preheated) 300° oven and bake,
stirring it after 30 minutes. Continue to bake for 1½ hours,
pour in cream, and bake 30 minutes more. Serve warm.

Asparagus Risotto

This risotto has a subtle, rich taste. Serve with a simple salad for a complete meal.

18 asparagus stalks

¾ cup unsalted butter

1 onion, cut into 1"–2" squares

2 cups uncooked Arborio rice

⅔ cup dry white wine

6–7 cups chicken stock

⅔ teaspoon dried thyme

⅔ cup freshly grated sharp Parmesan cheese

Freshly ground black pepper to taste

Trim the asparagus. If the stalks are slender, leave the tips whole; otherwise, cut in half lengthwise and then cut the stalks on the diagonal into pieces approximately 1" long. Set aside.

Melt ¾ of the butter in a large, heavy skillet. Turn the heat to low, add the onion, and stir until it begins to become transparent. Add the rice. Increase the heat to medium. Stir and try to coat each grain with butter; when the grains are shiny, pour in the wine and mix. When the mixture becomes dry, add a cup of stock; stir. Keep adding stock as needed and continue to stir, so no rice sticks to the bottom of the pot. After 10 minutes or so, add the asparagus and stir gently. Continue adding stock as needed. After about 4 minutes, add the thyme and stir. When the rice is finished cooking (about 4 minutes more) add the cheese and the remaining butter. Stir just until it melts. Season with black pepper and serve immediately.

Beancurd and Fried Rice

Zen practitioner and cookbook author David Scott suggests using cold leftover rice for this dish, not simply to avoid any waste, but also because when rice is cold, it can be coated in the oil more easily, thus preventing the grains from sticking together.

2 tablespoons oil

1 clove garlic, crushed

1 medium onion, diced

4 ounces mushrooms, sliced

4 ounces celery or green beans, chopped

1 pound cooked rice

6 ounces beancurd (tofu), cubed

1 egg

2 tablespoons soy sauce

Heat the oil in a heavy frying pan. Add the crushed garlic and onion. Sauté until the onions are just soft, and then add the mushrooms and celery or beans. Fry gently for 2–3 minutes. Stir in the rice and beancurd. Heat through, stirring constantly. Break the egg over the mixture, sprinkle on the soy sauce, and mix well. Serve immediately.

Note: For fried rice with a less creamy texture, replace the eggs with strips of omelet.

Tomato and Rice Soup

This tomato and rice soup recipe is satisfying in winter when you can use canned tomatoes and superb in summer when fresh tomatoes are abundant.

1 tablespoon good quality olive oil

1 medium onion, chopped

1 carrot, sliced

1 stalk celery, with leaves, chopped

3 cloves minced garlic

¾ cup uncooked brown rice

4 cups chopped tomatoes or 1 28-ounce can crushed
   tomatoes

1 teaspoon tomato paste

3 cups water

1 teaspoon salt

   Pepper to taste

1 tablespoon fresh basil or 1 teaspoon dried

   Pinch thyme and oregano

Heat the oil in a 3- to 4-quart, heavy-bottomed pot. Add onion, carrot, celery, and garlic, and sauté for about 5 minutes until onion is transparent. Add rice, stirring for about 5 minutes. Add tomatoes and remaining ingredients and bring to boil. Cover and simmer for about 50 minutes. To add more body to the soup, puree about 2 cups in a blender and return to pot. Adjust seasonings.

Break during sesshin.
Napping in the lounge. Wake up!
And smell the coffee.
—Sallie Tisdale

Buddha

The name Buddha *refers to the historical Buddha, or Shakyamuni Buddha, but* buddha *is also a general name for any enlightened being. In this commentary, Zen master Shunryu Suzuki stresses that practitioners must follow the Buddha's example and abandon ascetic idealistic practices in favor of moderation, discovering through trial and error by what means they can transform themselves into an enlightened being: "How this physical body becomes a sage is our main interest."*

The Indian thought and practice encountered by Buddha was based on an idea of human beings as a combination of spiritual and physical elements. They thought that the physical side of man bound the spiritual side, and so their religious practice was aimed at making the physical element weaker in order to free and strengthen the spirit. Thus the practice Buddha found in India emphasized asceticism. But Buddha found when he practiced asceticism that there was no limit to the attempt to purge ourselves physically, and that it made religious practice very idealistic. This kind of war with our body can only end when we die. But according to this Indian thought, we will return in another life, and another life, to repeat the struggle over and over again, without ever attaining perfect enlightenment. And even if you think you can make your physical strength weak enough to free your spiritual power, it will only work as long as you continue your ascetic practice. If you resume your everyday life you will have to strengthen your body, but then you will have to weaken it again to regain your spiritual power. And then you will have to repeat this process over and over again. This may be too great a simplification of the Indian practice encountered by Buddha, and we may laugh at it, but actually some people continue this practice even today. Sometimes without realizing it, this idea of asceticism is in the back of their minds. But practicing in this way will not result in any progress.

Buddha's way was quite different. At first he studied the Hindu practice of his time, and he practiced asceticism. But Buddha was not interested in the elements comprising human beings, nor in metaphysical theories of existence. He was more concerned about how he himself existed in this moment. That was his point. Bread is made from flour. How flour becomes bread when put in the oven was for Buddha the most important thing. How we become enlightened was his main interest. The enlightened person is some perfect, desirable character, for himself and for others. Buddha wanted to find out how human beings develop this ideal character—how various sages in the past became sages. In order to find out how dough became perfect bread, he made it over and over again, until he became quite successful. That was his practice.

But we may find it is not so interesting to cook the same thing over and over again every day. It is rather tedious, you may say. If you lose the spirit of repetition it will become quite difficult, but it will not be difficult if you are full of strength and vitality. Anyway, we cannot keep still; we have to do something. So if you do something, you should be very observant, and careful and alert. Our way is to put the dough in the oven and watch it carefully. Once you know how the dough becomes bread, you will understand enlightenment. So how this physical body becomes a sage is our main interest. We are not so concerned about what flour is, or what dough is, or what a sage is. A sage is a sage. Metaphysical explanations of human nature are not the point.

So the kind of practice we stress thus cannot become too idealistic. If an artist becomes too idealistic, he will commit suicide, because between his ideal and his actual ability there is a great gap. Because there is no bridge long enough to go across that gap, he will begin to despair. That is the usual spiritual way. But our spiritual way is not so idealistic. In some sense we should be idealistic; at least we should be interested in making bread which tastes good and looks good! Actual practice is repeating over and over again until you find out how to become bread. There is no secret in our way. Just to practice zazen [sitting meditation] and put ourselves into the oven is our way.

Focaccia

This traditional bread used to be baked on a hot stone in the ashes of the hearth, but a conventional oven works as well.

    1 cup lukewarm water
    1 package dry yeast (1/2 ounce)
    3 tablespoons olive oil
    2 teaspoons salt
    2–3 teaspoons fresh sage or 1 teaspoon dried sage
    2 cups whole wheat flour
    3 cups all-purpose flour
    Coarse sea salt, to taste

Mix water and yeast; let stand in the large bowl of an electric mixer about 5 minutes. Add oil, salt, and half of the sage and then stir in 2 cups of the flour. Beat well until dough is elastic, then add about ½ cup more flour (until stiff). Knead until smooth and elastic, adding flour as needed. Turn into an oiled bowl, cover with damp cloth, and let rise in warm place until doubled in size (1–3 hours).

Punch down dough and roll to fit into 11" x 15" shallow baking pan. With fingers, dimple dough at 1" intervals. Sprinkle with remaining sage and sea salt, and drizzle with a bit of olive oil.

Bake about 20 minutes till golden brown at 450°. Cut into strips and serve.

Puja Bread

M a k e s   1 8

A recipe for puja bread adapted by Betty Jung from Kopan, a Tibetan Buddhist monastery in Nepal. These chapatis are made especially for the puja (ritual offering) ceremonies at Kopan, where they are offered and then distributed and eaten during the feasting rite.

- 5 cups white flour
- 1 teaspoon baking powder
- ⅓ cup sugar
- ½ teaspoon salt
- 1¼ cups water
- ¼ cup vegetable oil

Pour flour in a mound on a counter or in a mixing bowl. Make a hole in the center. Sprinkle baking powder, sugar, and salt on top. Pour half the amount of warm water into the hole. With your hand, mix the dry ingredients from the top of the mound with the water. Work in a circular motion until mixed. Add the second half of the water and repeat the process. Add the oil and repeat the process until everything is thoroughly mixed. Knead well for at least 5 minutes. The dough should be well incorporated, not sticky. Cover and set aside 30 minutes. On a well-floured surface, knead the dough into a long sausage shape about 1½" in diameter. Cut into pieces 1" wide, or about the width of 2 fingers. Dust with flour and flatten each piece into a round shape with the palm of your hand. With a rolling pin, roll out to approximately 6" in diameter. Warm a cast-iron griddle or skillet over medium heat. Remove excess flour from the chapati by tossing it back and forth in your hands. Place one at a time on the hot griddle. Turn every 30–60 seconds. Cooking time should be 5–7 minutes. When cooked, the chapati should feel light. Undercooked ones will feel heavier.

Gingerbread

A *light, spicy dessert bread.*

⅔ cup sugar

⅔ cup molasses

⅔ cup boiling water

2 tablespoons butter

1 teaspoon baking soda

1 egg, well beaten

1½ cups flour

1 teaspoon cinnamon

1 teaspoon ginger

¼ teaspoon cloves

Mix ingredients, pour into a square pan, and bake in an oven preheated to 350° until bread springs back to touch.

Serve warm, with freshly whipped cream if desired.

Challah

Challah bread is a sweet egg bread and a symbol of life in the Jewish tradition.

5–6 cups sifted flour
3 tablespoons sugar
1½ teaspoons salt
1 package dry yeast (¼ ounce)
½ cup softened butter
1 pinch powdered saffron
1 cup warm water
4 eggs at room temperature
1 teaspoon cold water
1 teaspoon poppy seeds

Combine 1 cup of flour with the sugar, salt, and yeast in a large bowl. Mix in the butter. Dissolve saffron in warm water and add a little at a time to flour mixture. Beat 2 minutes at medium speed with electric mixer. Separate 1 egg, reserving yolk. Add white and other 3 eggs into batter with another ½ cup of flour and beat on high for another 2 minutes. Blend in additional flour as needed to make a soft dough. Knead on floured surface for 10 minutes until silky and elastic. Put into greased bowl, turning to coat top, and cover with damp cloth. Put in warm place for about 1 hour to double.

Punch down and divide into 6 equal pieces. Roll each piece into a rectangle and then roll rectangle into a cylinder, continuing to roll until you get 12" ropes. Attach 3 ropes by pinching the ends together, and turn under. Braid and turn under other end. Place on oiled baking sheet and brush with oil. Let rise again in warm, draft-free place, and preheat oven to 400°. Mix egg yolk with 1 teaspoon water and brush loaves with this mixture and sprinkle with poppy seed. Bake 20–25 minutes. Cool on wire racks.

Ritual is about joining vision and practicality, heaven and earth, samsara and nirvana. When things are properly understood, one's whole life is like a ritual or a ceremony. . . . [Chogyam Trungpa] Rinpoche often said that the dharma, the teachings of the Buddha, are like a recipe for fresh-baked bread. Thousands of years ago someone discovered how to bake bread, and because the recipe was passed down for years and years, you can still make fresh bread that you can eat right now.
—Ane Pema Chodron

Changes

Composer John Cage celebrated spontaneous changes through his chance compositions. The music encouraged people to recognize and appreciate the sounds that occurred naturally around them. His ideas were influenced by his study of Zen Buddhism with D. T. Suzuki; Cage attended his lectures at Columbia University from 1949 to 1951. Through his music, Cage introduced many listeners to Buddhist views. When Cage's health began to *deteriorate in the mid-1970s as a result of his rich diet and demanding schedule, he was referred to Shizuko Yamamoto, a Shiatsu practitioner and macrobiotic specialist who helped him transform his health through diet. Cage shared his thoughts on changes in nutrition and its connection to personal transformation in an interview conducted by Francine Schiff.*

C hange is the nature of the universe, but to consciously transform yourself is not so simple. The music was always changing long ago. But music is a special circumstance, which we do as though we were exercising the mind. Music is like sitting square-legged. It's special. You can do very difficult things in music that you don't yet do in your life.

But when you get involved directly with things like food changing your personality, you're much closer to daily life. Disciplines in the field of music are simple, but getting them into our daily lives is more difficult. . . .

When I first went to Shizuko, she said to me, "Eat when you're hungry, and drink when you're thirsty. Don't drink unless you are thirsty, and don't eat unless you are hungry." I liked what she said, although I didn't fully understand it. I don't think I do yet. It sounded like someone saying, shiver in the winter, perspire in the summer. It sounded straight-forward.

But we don't really know when we're hungry. We tend to think that we ought to be hungry in the morning, at noon, and in the evening, but maybe we're not hungry. Maybe we're eating simply out of habit. Maybe we're hungry at some other time. In solitude, we can learn when we are hungry. I'm actually trying to find out when I am alone, whether or not I am hungry or thirsty. I can tell thirst more easily than I can tell hunger, because when you are thirsty your mouth gets dry. But

I can't quite tell what hunger is, because I eat too much. Hunger must be an empty stomach, it must slightly hurt. Hunger and emptiness are related. But I'm very apt to eat before I'm hungry, because I still eat according to the hour, rather than what I truly feel. Solitude can teach us when we are hungry on every level. But I'm perfectly happy to be talking about food.

My personality is changing due to what I am eating. I am calmer altogether, perhaps a little bit too calm. And how I'm going to change that, I don't yet know. But I'm pretty sure that it could be changed more effectively through food, than through any other means . . .

My diet is basically brown rice and some beans, either the black beans, or kidney beans, or garbanzo beans, or lima beans. And it's a lot of seeds. Like sunflower seeds, sesame seeds, and sometimes those pumpkin seeds. Then I love to make the Tibetan barley bread that you can find in *The Tassajara Bread Book*. I enjoy working with it; kneading it is so relaxing. Finally it becomes less gluey and pasty and falling apart, and it becomes itself, it becomes a thing. It can take whatever form you give it.

John Cage's Brown Rice

I make brown rice in a pressure cooker because it seals in the nutrients. Covers on most pots are not as tight as the pressure cooker and keeping the steam in is the secret of getting it right. [Vitamin] B and all other nutrients in the rice rather than in the air . . . The other thing I do is use fresh spring water. I go out to the country and get it myself . . . I put the water into those gallon bottles that you get apple juice in. The spring water usually comes from Long Island, in Locust Valley, or I get it at Stony Point. I enjoy making the special trip to go out and get the water. And on the way I might find some mushrooms, or I might solve a problem in my work, because my mind would be off my work . . .

It is easy to make the basic brown rice, and once it's made you can add herbs and nuts, whatever. It's two cups of rice, which you wash, and put into a pressure cooker. Add a tablespoonful of soy sauce, or you could use the same amount of sea salt. Then you use three cups of spring water. Put in the pressure cooker over a high flame, and when it comes to its steaming point, put the heat on low, slip an asbestos pad underneath it, and simmer for about 40 minutes.

John Cage's Kidney Beans with Herbs

1 cup kidney beans

3 cups water

1 teaspoon soy sauce

1 tablespoon cumin seeds

I don't cook the beans in the pressure cooker, just rice. I soak the beans overnight. Then I bring them to a boil for ten minutes, reduce the heat, and cook them until they are tender. I try one way or another to get rid of the liquid, to get them near dryness, so that the amount of liquid is like a sauce. I add soy sauce, and in the beginning of cooking might add some herb. This especially enhances the kidney beans. I like to put in cumin seeds, which I toast before I use, in a frying pan. The herbs get more fragrance that way. You just throw the seeds into the pan for a few minutes, without using any oil, because the seeds already have oil in them.

A Retreat Tortilla

A retreat recipe to help settle body and mind from monk Michael Roach:

"On long-term retreats, food is very important. The wrong kind or quantity of food can lead to serious problems during meditation. Each person's physical constitution is different, in every case it is essential to eat well and avoid extremes that would affect the mind during meditation. Foods that overly stimulate the body should be strictly avoided: coffee, sweets, and soft drinks are obvious examples. I find that fresh vegetables and juices without sugar help the mind focus. This is a dish I discovered once during a wonderful long retreat in my childhood home in the Arizona desert."

> 1 fresh zucchini
> Monterey Jack cheese
> Butter
> 3 large flour tortillas
> Some fresh local salsa

Cut the zucchini into round slices, and the cheese into slabs. Put a few slabs of butter in a frying pan, and cook until clarified (clear liquid just short of burning). This clarified butter is an important ingredient in many dishes used by Tibetan monk meditators to aid digestion. Put a tortilla in the pan, place slabs of cheese on half of it. When the cheese has melted spread the zucchini slices over the cheese; spoon salsa over the zucchini. Quickly fold over the tortilla, in half, and continue to cook for about a minute. Eat while warm.

Funny Stuff

Serves 1

James Thornton, an environmental lawyer turned teacher of contemplative practice to activists and policymakers, offers a breakfast that doubles as a preventative medicine:

"Here's my favorite breakfast, an ayurvedic [Indian yogic] offering that we call 'funny stuff' at home. The heart of the recipe is turmeric, meant to be the most powerful root according to the ayurveda, cleansing the organs, lubricating the joints, and boosting immune functions. Eat it every morning during flu season."

Chop a 1-inch cube of gingerroot; sauté the ginger in about 1 tablespoon olive oil, until slightly soft; add 1 tablespoon turmeric, and cook for 8 minutes to release the medicinal value (a bit of water may be added as it cooks); take off heat. Add 5 nuts of your choice, and a cup of yogurt. Mix evenly, and enjoy.

A BUDDHIST MEAL BLESSING

The Venerable Ayya Khema offers the following verses on obser-
vance at a meal, which she describes as the Buddha's words and says
"are meant to remind us that we are eating to survive well and not
just for reasons of pleasing the palate."

We are eating this meal with mindfulness
Not only for pleasure, not for indulgence,
but only for maintaining this body,
so that it endures.
For keeping it unharmed,
for supporting life,
so that former feelings of hunger are destroyed
and new feelings from overeating do not arise,
then there will be a lack of bodily obstacles
and living comfortably.

Dharma

Dharma *is a Sanskrit word that can be translated as "ultimate reality," as the teaching of the Buddha's truth, or as all phenomena. The revered thirteenth-century Zen master Dogen wrote, "Dharma is eating and eating is dharma." This statement, or koan, has been examined by Zen masters for centuries. Here Zen master John Daido Loori takes this koan as the starting point for a discourse on eating and interconnectedness. He invokes an*

image that recurs frequently in Buddhist texts: the net of Indra,
the jeweled heavenly web in which each star is said to contain the
reflection of every other star in the firmament, every part
containing the whole. The net of Indra is a metaphor for every
living thing in relationship to all other phenomena, everything
bound up in the web of all dharmas.

This passage follows the traditional format for koan
commentary.

The Prologue

Heaven cannot cover it. The earth cannot support it. Space cannot accommodate it. The sun and moon cannot illuminate it. If you have not as yet realized it, then straight away cut off all complications and clinging and see directly that every Dharma in this precious life is practice. That each and every object and action release the great shining illumination. Only then will you be independent and free in the midst of phenomena. Whatever you take up, there is nothing that is not it.

But tell me, "What is attained that is so extraordinary?"
"If you have not yet understood it, listen to this old teaching."

The Main Case

The great master Dogen taught the practice of eating is the essential truth of all Dharmas. At the very moment of eating we merge with ultimate reality. Thus, Dharma is eating, and eating is Dharma and this eating is full of holy joy and ecstasy.

The Capping Verse

Take off the blinders, set down the pack, free of any encumbrance journey straight ahead deep into the recesses of the hundred thousand mountains and valleys. Among falling blossoms and flowing streams no trace of passing remains.

What is it that's attained that's extraordinary? It's one thing to understand that every Dharma in this precious life is practice. It's easy enough to understand. It's easy enough to believe. But understanding it and believing it won't cut it. It's only when that fact is realized, when you make it your own, that truly every Dharma, every action is practice.

Because food is what it is, it is of utmost importance that we receive it with deep gratitude, because we consume life. Whether it's cabbages or cows, it's life that we consume. There isn't a meal that's taken by any creature large or small on the face of this great Earth that's not done except at the expense of another creature's life. That's the nature of life on the planet Earth. We nourish and sustain each other with our lives. How can we not be grateful for the life that sustains us? How can we not wish to give back to the ten thousand things that which we receive? And it's in that process that the sacredness of taking a meal is revealed, that the truth of the ten thousand Dharmas is revealed. This statement of Dogen's was from the *Vimalakirti Sutra* and in the *Vimalakirti Sutra* it is said that when a person is enlightened in their eating, all things are enlightened as well. If all Dharmas are nondual, the person is also nondual in their eating. Dogen goes on to elaborate on that basic statement in the *Vimalakirti Sutra*. He says indeed, Dharma is identified with one's eating and one's eating is identified with Dharma, for this reason: if Dharma is the Dharma-nature, a meal is also the Dharma-nature. And you need understand that Dharma is one of the three treasures of Buddhism: Buddha, Dharma, and Sangha. Buddha treasure is the historical Buddha, but it's also all sentient beings. Buddha means enlightened one. Dharma is the teachings of the Buddha and at the same time Dharma is the ten thousand things, the whole phenomenal universe is called Dharma. And sangha is the community of practitioners of the Buddha's Dharma and at once all sentient beings. So Buddha, Dharma, and Sangha are at once the individual and the whole phenomenal universe. And so when he talks about Dharma-nature here he's talking about the teachings Dharma and the whole phenomenal universe Dharma. For this reason if Dharma is the Dharma-nature, a meal also is the Dharma-nature. If Dharma is thusness, food is likewise thusness. If Dharma is one mind, a meal is also one mind. If Dharma is enlightenment, food is enlightenment. Therefore the act of eating constitutes the truth of all Dharmas. This can fully be comprehended only by and among buddhas, that is enlightened beings, at the very moment when we eat we are possessed of ultimate reality, essence, substance, energy, activity, causation, so Dharma is eating and eating is Dharma. And this Dharma is enjoyed by Buddhas of past and future, this eating is full of holy joy and ecstasy. At the very moment we eat, we're possessed of ultimate reality, essence, substance, energy, activity, causation. That is we merge with the whole phenomenal universe. We're in a dynamic relationship with the whole phenomenal universe.

The little scientific fantasy I've often had is that if the water, just the water, on this mountain were tagged with heavy hydrogen, that is instead of H_2O it would be D_2O, in a very short period of time you would find D_2O in the plants that are growing in the garden, in the grasses, in the deer, in the raccoons and the birds and the eagles. You'd find it in the people. Not only that it would be in our breath. It would be in our urine. It would be in the water that flows to New York City and comes out the faucets in New York City, it would be in New Zealand and Japan. It would be in Alaska. Each time a person would come here and consume a meal with this deuterium in this water they would take it back to wherever they go and enter into the incredible biological equilibrium of that system, and soon, in a very short period of time, it would reach everywhere. Well, that's the way it is. It reaches everywhere. We reach everywhere. Past, present, and future. There's no way by any stretch of the imagination, scientifically or spiritually that we can separate ourselves from this Earth, from this universe. And so when we take a meal we enter into that process again and again of merging with everything that surrounds us. When we use the lavatory we enter into the process of merging with everything that surrounds us. When we breathe in and out that dynamic equilibrium that's the great diamond net of Indra is activated and we become part of the whole universe. When we realize it with our mind, we merge.

So eating becomes a celebration of the Dharma with no separation between eating and samadhi [serene, collected state of mind], the samadhi of self-fulfillment, the samadhi of play, the samadhi of self-fulfilling activity. We take that food in the bowl. We call the bowl the Buddha's bowl. Master Dogen said the Buddha bowl is not an artifact. It neither arises nor perishes, neither comes nor goes, neither gains nor loses, it is not concerned with past, present, or future. This bowl is called the miraculous utensil. Miraculous because it's used in a miraculous event in a miraculous time by a miraculous person. On this account where a miraculous event is realized there is a miraculous bowl. There's no need to *search* for the miraculous. We're surrounded by it. Interpenetrated by it. Our very life is a manifestation of that miraculousness.

Free-Range Coq au Vin

1   large free-range chicken, cut into 6 or 8 pieces
2   tablespoons flour
3   tablespoons butter
1   tablespoon plus four teaspoons vegetable oil
¼   pound lean bacon, cut in 1-inch pieces
1   medium onion, quartered
1   carrot, peeled and quartered
1   stick celery, tough fibers removed and cut into thirds
2½   cups full-bodied red wine
4   tablespoons brandy
1   clove garlic
     Bouquet garni (fines herbes wrapped in cheese cloth)
1   teaspoon plus one pinch sugar
18–20   small (pearl) onions
½   pound button mushrooms, halved
     Salt, to taste
     Freshly ground black pepper, to taste
1½   tablespoons chopped parsley

Season 2 tablespoons of the flour with salt and pepper. Toss the chicken pieces in the flour. Melt 1 tablespoon of butter with 1 tablespoon oil in a heavy pot over medium heat. Add the chicken, fry gently until browned on all sides. Remove the chicken pieces to a warmed plate. Add the bacon, the medium-sized onion, carrot, and celery and sauté until tender.

Heat the brandy in a small saucepan. Return the chicken pieces to the pot. Pour the brandy over the chicken and ignite (with a match) shaking the pan so that all of the chicken pieces are covered in flames. Wait until the flames are extinguished (a few seconds) and pour the wine (reserving 1 tablespoon for later use) into the pot and stir. Add the garlic, bouquet garni, and the teaspoon of sugar, to the mixture and bring to a boil, cover and simmer until tender (1 to 1½ hours). While the chicken is cooking melt another tablespoon of butter with 2 teaspoons of oil in a skillet. Fry the small onions in the oil until lightly browned; add the pinch of sugar, one tablespoon wine, and one tablespoon water. Cover and simmer until the onions are barely tender; remove from heat and cover. Melt 1 tablespoon of butter with 2 remaining teaspoons of oil; add the mushrooms and cook for a few minutes.

When the chicken is finished, remove the pieces from the pot and place on a serving platter; arrange the onions and mushrooms around the chicken. Cover and keep hot; remove the bouquet garni and bring the sauce to a boil; reduce until thickened, season to taste, strain the sauce and pour over the chicken. Garnish with parsley and serve.

Christina Feldman, a teacher of insight meditation, offers guidelines for mindful eating as well as a recipe.

B ringing mindfulness and sensitivity into our times of eating transforms them into moments of grace and connectedness. Each time we eat with mindfulness, we nourish not only our bodies but also our hearts. A moment of sensitivity when eating alone reminds us to be present on our Earth with appreciation and respect. When sharing meals with others in a climate of mindfulness, they become moments of pausing in our lives, sharing not only food but warmth of heart.

Lentil Soup

1 onion

3 carrots, chopped

4 stalks celery, chopped

   Olive oil

1 tablespoon cumin powder

1 cup red split lentils

1 small can tomatoes or 4 chopped tomatoes

3 cups water

1 teaspoon salt

1 teaspoon soy sauce

3 tablespoons dried chopped coriander leaf or fresh
   coriander

½ teaspoon pepper

Sauté onion, carrots, and celery in a little olive oil for a few
minutes. Then add the remaining ingredients. Let it all simmer for 45 minutes to 1 hour. Adjust seasonings and water.
Play with adding other vegetables. Serve with warm bread.

Guidelines for Mindful Eating

- Resolve not to eat when standing or walking. Take the time to eat and be still.
- Resolve to take only what your body needs. Remind yourself that as we serve ourselves, we nourish and care for our bodies and can never fill the never-satisfied mind.
- As we prepare or wait for food to be served, take these moments to connect with our bodies and listen well to the moment.
- As you sit to eat, take a few moments to reflect with gratitude upon the efforts and labor of the many people who have been involved in providing us with this food.
- Reflect upon the nature of the interdependence that lies between ourselves and the Earth.
- As you eat, bring a wholehearted attentiveness to taste, to smell, to sensation.
- As you finish your meal, take a moment to extend appreciation and lovingkindness to yourself, to those you care for, and to those who care for you, to all beings, known and unknown. May all live in peace.

"ONE SHOULD NOT TALK TO A SKILLED HUNTER
ABOUT WHAT IS FORBIDDEN BY THE BUDDHA"
—HSYIANG-YEN

A gray fox, female, nine pounds three ounces.
39⅝" long with tail.
Peeling skin back (Kai
reminded us to chant the Shingyo first)
cold pelt, crinkle; and musky smell
mixed with dead-body odor starting.
Stomach content: a whole ground squirrel well chewed
plus one lizard foot
and somewhere from inside the ground squirrel
a bit of aluminum foil

The secret.
and the secret hidden deep in that.
—Gary Snyder

Ego

Diminishing the hold of the ego—*I want, I desire, I need*—is a central aspect of Buddhist practice. When preparing food, one of the greatest challenges is to cook without concern for an ego reward—that is to just cook without thought of praise or reward. The Zen cook aims simply to become one with the act of cooking itself. Pat Enkyo O'Hara, ordained in the Soto tradition and a professor of interactive telecommunications at New York

University, reflects on learning to cook by simply responding to a given situation, by paying attention only to what is appropriate.

> To carry the self forward and realize the ten thousand dharmas is delusion. That the ten thousand dharmas advance and realize the self is enlightenment.
>
> —from Dogen Zenji's *Genjokoan*, translation by Maezumi Roshi

I t is odd how some very delicious meals seem to have no authorship and other ones seem to scream, "Look how clever I am!" If you've cooked very much, you've undoubtedly experienced both kinds of cooking. Typically, there are those wonderfully creative moments of flow in the kitchen when everything seems right—and then that moment when flow stops and some awkward, arch, or stilted thing emerges. We can see it in art and in writing, in all aspects of life; it is that self-consciousness that is a fixed notion of the self, going out to impose itself on the universe rather than be confirmed by the universe.

It's such a subtle thing, that difference, which starts somewhere in the breath, in the mind, and then spreads out to everything we touch. The difference between reaching out with "my" idea of what to cook or how to cook, and instead to allow food and cooking to, as Dogen says, "realize the self."

It is not just a question of flow, either. Rather, this approach to cooking arises out of a profoundly different sense of our relation to the universe. It is my Zen practice that helps me see the difference.

Long before I started Buddhist practice, cooking had always settled me down, allowed me to simply be in each moment. Whether baking bread or reducing a sauce, I enjoyed the purely physical process of cooking, slicing and chopping by hand for the sheer sensual encounter with texture, fragrance, color, and shape. Not only did I take pleasure in cooking, but also in serving an uncommon, delicious meal to others. I loved to delight my family and friends with insistent spices, rare flavors, the unusual in aroma, texture, temperature. There was a joy in giving, and certainly an enjoyment of cooking and a pleasure in my reputation as a good cook.

After a few years of Zen practice, it began to fall to me to prepare meals during retreats. I was excited at the prospect of presenting some extraordinary delicacies that would dramatically contrast with our black oryoki bowls and would tempt the palate of our retreatants, tease, and delight their senses. I would really demonstrate what awareness and mindfulness in the kitchen could produce!

But as I began to plan menus, an odd thing happened: I realized how inappropriate were the impressive menus I had in mind. I needed to think differently about it.

Wasn't it more appropriate to notice what food was available? (It was a cold New York winter.) And the situation? (A New York City sangha who typically had access to every kind of food imaginable.)

My impressive ideas about cooking began to slip away. Didn't I simply want to provide an appropriate meal that would call no attention to the food or the cook? In fact, in this case, wouldn't a simple meal be more suitable to the context of a retreat? And I began to see the whole function of the cook in a different way. The cook must be awake and responsive to the needs of the group: meals that steady a nervous group, that enliven the sluggish, that feed us all without distraction. That these meals are appropriate to the circumstances, that they are an advancing of the "ten thousand dharmas" doesn't make them less delicious or varied or playful. It is more that the elements of the world come and connect with the cook and out of that is created the meal that serves all sentient beings.

So that's how I came to personally hear Dogen Zenji's couplet in *Genjokoan*:

"To carry the self forward and realize the ten thousand dharmas is delusion. That the ten thousand dharmas advance and realize the self is enlightenment."

The recipes below are all from Pat Enkyo O'Hara.

Quick and Tasty Broth for Noodles or Vegetables

1   1" x 1" square of kombu, or other sturdy seaweed

3   dried shiitake mushrooms (or boletus, etc.)

5   cups water

3   tablespoons tamari

    Green onions, chopped (to taste)

Place seaweed and mushrooms in a pan with some water. Let it slowly come to simmer. Simmer gently 5 minutes; remove seaweed and mushrooms. Remove tough center of mushrooms, chop, and return to broth. Kombu can be sliced and returned to broth or discarded. Add tamari to taste, pour over cooked noodles, and top with chopped green onions.

Variations

- Use stock, not water.
- Add 2 tablespoons mirin or sherry or 1 tablespoon sesame oil to simmering broth.
- With tamari, add fresh ginger, peeled and sliced into tiny matchsticks.

Pressed Salad

A *light and cool salad that keeps for several days.*

½ Chinese cabbage

5 globe radishes, sliced

1 tender carrot, sliced

A few sprigs of Italian parsley, stems removed

1 tablespoon each of umeboshi vinegar, soy sauce,
toasted sesame oil, and mixed peppercorns (red,
green, and black)

Mix all ingredients together in a glass or plastic bowl. Either
use a vegetable press* or place a plate or other cover on top of
the cabbage and weigh it down with a heavy object (a heavy
rock or a pot of water). Let the cabbage press for an hour. Remove the weight, toss the salad, and serve.

---

*An inexpensive vegetable press made of plastic and a tighten-down top can be found
in most Asian markets. It is great for all kinds of vegetable pickles.

Apple Crisp

A p p l e   M i x t u r e
- 8 apples
- 1 cup water
-    Pinch sea salt
- ½ cup currants
- 2 tablespoons kuzu, or potato starch if not available

Peel and slice apples, combine with water and sea salt, and bring to a boil. Cover; simmer over low heat about 5 minutes, but don't let the apples get too soft. Add the currants and kuzu diluted in 2 tablespoons of water. Stir constantly until kuzu thickens and clarifies. Pour into baking dish.

T h e   C r i s p
- 1 cup rolled oats
- ½ cup almonds
- ¼ cup sunflower seeds
- ¼ cup walnuts
-    Pinch sea salt
- 2 tablespoons rice syrup or honey

Toast the oats in a dry iron skillet until brown. (Be careful! It's easy to burn them.) Transfer to a bowl. Toast each of the nuts separately, chop the almonds and walnuts, and mix with the oats. Add a pinch of salt and the rice syrup or honey. Stir together and spread the crisp over the apples. Cook in 300° oven for 15 minutes or until brown. Cool.

Under the cherry—
blossom soup,
blossom salad.
—Basho, translated by Lucien Stryk

Feast

Feasting, in particular celebrating sacred feast offerings, comprises an essential part of tantric Buddhist practice. Tantra is a branch of Buddhism concerned with transforming every encounter—pleasant or unpleasant, pure or impure—into the spiritual path. Originating in ancient India, tantric feast celebrations may seem remote or even bizarre, but they function as a "mystery rite" that frees participants from ordinary dualistic perceptions. According to

Lama Surya Das, participating in a feast "genuinely transforms the way we experience the world." Consequently, advanced practitioners are completely liberated from ordinary limited perceptions and consume everything with equal delight, whether it be poison or nectar. Here, Lama Surya Das describes the tantric feast offering known in Tibetan as tsok, which translates as gathering.

What is gathered? First, we gather the feast of dakas and dakinis: the yogis and yoginis who share our practice and vows. Second, we gather all the sacred substances and sense-pleasures: food and drink, costumes and ornaments, song and dance, flowers, lamps, and so on. Third, we invoke the meditational deities and Dharma Protectors as well as arranging holy images and other power objects and ritual instruments. Fourth, we gather merit—the good karma accumulated as spiritual rewards for wholesome, spiritual activities.

An indispensable part of the offering is the five meats and five nectars, which help practitioners to transcend conceptual discrimination and thus deepen, or accumulate, Gnostic awareness. Offered and celebrated are disgusting as well as delectable things, thus overcoming conceptual limitations. These two groups of substances are intended to symbolically represent the inseparability of wisdom and compassion—truth and unconditional love—in the awakened heart-mind.

The five meats are traditionally beef, elephant meat, horse meat, dog, and human flesh. The five nectars are traditionally milk, yogurt, blood, semen, and alcoholic beverages. These may be offered symbolically, through rites including sacred homemade pills, rather than in material form. They can also be offered as *tormas*—literally, that which scatters egotism. Tormas are most often cone-shaped ritual offering cakes made of *tsampa* (dried, roasted barley flour) and butter or ghee, embodying the tantric principle of liquid and solid—method and wisdom, god and goddess inseparable in nondual embrace—in symbolic form. Sacred feasts, known as *ganachakra puja* (Sanskrit) or *tsok*, are offered most often on auspicious calendar days, such as the full and new moon, and on the anniversaries of the death of enlightened masters and lineage holders.

How are they actually practiced? First, those initiates assembled offer bows to the Buddha and his present embodiment (the guru actually present); then they raise selfless *bodhicitta*, or enlightened mind, through meditation. Prayers are then chanted and liturgies recited to invoke all the enlightened ones—from all the ten directions, and of the past, present, and future—to come as guests, inviting all the innumerable Buddhas, Bodhisattvas, dakas, dakinis, and guardians of the sublime Dharma.

First, we offer the objects delightful to the six senses to celebrate all sense experience as the display of nondual awareness. Second, confession of all evil actions is made through offering consecrated substances and nectar. Third, obstacles and hindrances are offered to clear the path for one and all.

All the material offerings gathered on the altar—meats and nectars—are spiritually transformed into wisdom through mantra and visualizations, mudras, and principally through *samadhi*. Practitioners then partake of the transubstantiated offering substances, which have been previously offered to the invited, visualized deities. The elixir of wisdom, the *dudtsi*, is distributed from the brimming ritual skullcup [a cup made from a human skull, a symbol of impermanence] from the altar, and the delicacies are also passed out and imbibed as spiritual sacraments. At this point, the celebrants are exhorted to perform spontaneous songs of enlightenment, vajra dances, and other passionate activities, in the realization that sensual delights are all offerings to the Buddha within each of us. Then the remainders of the feast are distributed.

BLESSING TO CHANT

What follows is a traditional, abbreviated form of the ganachakra puja, *translated by Lama Surya Das.*

In order to transform each meal into a vajra feast and every day into an auspicious one, do this:

1. Chant—Rahm, Yahm, Kahm! . . . Thus purifying each and every morsel with the sacred elemental energies of fire, water, and wind.
2. Chant—Om, Ah, Hung! . . . Thus blessing the food and transforming it into ambrosial wisdom-nectar, through with the sacred mantric seed-syllables embodying enlightened vajra-body, enlightened vajra-speech, and enlightened vajra-mind, and offering it to the inner deities within our own vajra body.
3. Feed the blessed food offerings like elixir to the deities residing within the mandala of oneself.

Sukiyaki

This dish is most enjoyable when the guests cook it together.

2 pounds sirloin, sliced paper thin

3 bunches green onion

1 bunch edible chrysanthemum or other edible green
such as broccoli rabe or watercress

12 shiitake mushrooms, trimmed

2 cakes firm bean curd cut in 1" squares
Optional: shirataki (white yam noodles, available
in cans at most Asian grocery stores)

Broth

1 cup sake (or water)

¼ cup soy sauce

1 teaspoon sugar

Arrange ingredients attractively on platters. Use an electric wok or a frying pan, placing it in center of table. Bring broth to simmer in pan—there will be just a little liquid in the bottom of the pan. Each guest is invited to put into the pan the ingredients he or she would like. The beef should take just a minute or so, the vegetables more or less time, to taste.

Tibetan Butter Tea

A recipe by Marilyn Stablein.

1 tablespoon loose tea leaves (preferably a smoky black tea)

¼ cup half-and-half (or half cream and half milk)

1 tablespoon butter

Salt

Boil tea in 4 cups of water for about 10 minutes. Remove from flame. Remove the tea leaves from the liquid by pouring through a sieve. Add half-and-half and butter to the strained tea. Add salt to taste. (Tibetans like it very salty!) This will cool the tea, so warm it briefly over a low flame, making sure the tea doesn't boil. For a frothy tea, pour it back and forth between two containers a few times.

Grace

Zen practitioner and Pulitzer Prize–winning poet Gary Snyder on the importance of grace:

T here is a verse chanted by Zen Buddhists called the "Four Great Vows." The first line goes: "Sentient beings are numberless, I vow to save them." *Shujo muhen seigando.* It's a bit daunting to announce this intention—aloud—to the universe daily. This vow stalked me for several years and finally pounced: I realized that I had vowed to let the sentient beings save *me*. In a similar way, the precept against taking life, against causing harm, doesn't stop in the negative. It is urging us to *give* life, to *undo* harm.

Those who attain some ultimate understanding of these things are called "Buddhas," which means "awakened ones." The word is connected to the English verb "to bud." I once wrote a little parable:

Who the Buddhas Are

All the beings of the universe are already realized. That is, with the exception of one or two beings. In those rare cases the cities, villages, meadows, and forests, with all their birds, flowers, animals, rivers, trees, and humans, that surround such a person, all collaborate to educate, serve, challenge, and instruct such a one, until that person also becomes a New Beginner Enlightened Being. Recently realized beings are enthusiastic to teach and train and start schools and practices. Being able to do this develops their confidence and insight up to the point that they are fully ready to join the seamless world of interdependent play. Such new enlightened beginners are called "Buddhas" and they like to say things like "I am enlightened together with the whole universe" and so forth.

—Boat in a Storm, 1987

"Good luck!" One might say. The test of the pudding is in the *eating*. It narrows down to a look at the conduct that is entwined with food. At mealtime (seated on the floor in lines) the Zen monks chant:

Porridge is effective in ten ways
To aid the student of Zen

No limit to the good result
Consummating eternal happiness

and

Oh, all you demons and spirits
We now offer this food to you
May all of you everywhere
Share it with us together

and

We wash our bowls in this water
It has the flavor of ambrosial dew
We offer it to all demons and spirits
May all be filled and satisfied
Om makula sai svaha

And several other verses. These superstitious-sounding old ritual formulas are never mentioned in lectures, but they are at the heart of the teaching. Their import is older than Buddhism or any of the world religions. They are part of the first and last practice of the wild: *Grace*.

Everyone who ever lived took the lives of other animals, pulled plants, plucked fruit, and ate. Primary people have had their own ways of trying to understand the precept of nonharming. They knew that taking life required gratitude and care. There is no death that is not somebody's food, no life that is not somebody's death. Some would take this as a sign that the universe is fundamentally flawed. This leads to a disgust with self, with humanity, and with nature. Otherworldly philosophies end up doing more damage to the planet (and human psyches) than the pain and suffering that is in the existential conditions they seek to transcend.

The archaic religion is to kill god and eat him. Or her. The shimmering food-chain, the food-web, is the scary, beautiful condition of the biosphere. Subsistence people live without excuses. The blood is on your own hands as you divide the liver from the gallbladder. You have watched the color fade on the glimmer of the trout. A subsistence economy is a sacramental economy because it has faced up to one of the critical problems of life and death: the taking of life for food. Contemporary people do not need to hunt, many cannot even afford meat, and in the developed world the variety of foods available to us makes the avoidance of meat an easy choice. Forests in the tropics are cut to make pasture to raise beef for the American market. Our distance from the source of our food enables us to be superficially more comfortable, and distinctly more ignorant.

Eating is a sacrament. The grace we say clears our hearts and guides the children and welcomes the guest, all at the same time. We look at eggs, apples, and stew. They are evidence of plenitude, excess, a great reproductive exuberance. Millions of grains of grass seed that will become rice or flour, millions of codfish fry that will never, and must never, grow to maturity. Innumerable little seeds are sacrifices to the food-chain. A parsnip in the ground is a marvel of living chemistry, making sugars and flavors from earth, air, water. And if we do eat meat it is the life, the bounce, the swish, of a great alert being with keen ears and lovely eyes, with foursquare feet and a huge beating heart that we eat, let us not deceive ourselves.

We too will be offerings—we are all edible. And if we are not devoured quickly, we are big enough (like the old down trees) to provide a long slow meal to the smaller critters. Whale carcasses that sink several miles deep in the ocean feed organisms in the dark for fifteen years. (It seems to take about two thousand to exhaust the nutrients in a high civilization.)

At our house we say a Buddhist grace—

We venerate the Three Treasures [teachers, the wild, and
    friends]
And are thankful for this meal
The work of many people
And the sharing of other forms of life.

Anyone can use a grace from their own tradition (and really give it meaning)—or make up their own. Saying some sort of grace is never inappropriate, and speeches and announcements can be tacked onto it. It is a plain, ordinary, old-fashioned little thing to do that connects us with all our ancestors.

Here follow recipes from some ancestors.

Laura Carter Holloway
Langford's Canned Corn

Born *in Nashville, Tennessee, in 1848, Laura Carter Holloway Langford published* The Buddhist Diet Book *in 1886, a vegetarian cookbook that aimed to help people eat a sensible vegetarian diet.*

To one can of corn add a cup of milk, a little salt, pepper, and butter, and scald, but do not boil.

Grammy's Butter Cookies

*W*ell *into her late eighties, my grandmother continued making these cookies for the people who lived on the third floor of her apartment building. Her neighbors encouraged her by leaving anonymous gifts of a pound of butter or a bag of sugar just outside her door.*

    1 cup softened butter
  1½ cups sugar
    2 eggs
    1 teaspoon vanilla extract
    3 cups sifted flour
    ½ teaspoon baking soda

Cream butter and sugar, add eggs, and beat until light and fluffy. Add vanilla. Sift flour and soda togther and add to creamed mixture. Chill dough for 3–4 hours. Roll on a floured surface, using as little flour as possible. Cut with cookie cutters. Sprinkle with crystallized brown sugar for decoration, if desired. Bake at 375° in a preheated oven for 6–8 minutes. Watch closely because they burn very quickly.

Indian Pudding

Serves 4 – 6

This is the classic New England recipe.

2 cups cold milk

¼ cup yellow cornmeal

2 cups scalded milk

½ cup best dark molasses

1 teaspoon salt

¼ cup sugar

1 teaspoon cinnamon

3 tablespoons butter

Mix ¼ cup cold milk with cornmeal. Stir into scalded milk and cook over hot water 20 minutes, stirring frequently. Add molasses, salt, sugar, cinnamon, and butter. Pour into buttered baking dish. Pour 1¾ cups cold milk over the top. Bake at 250° for 3 hours. Let stand ½ hour and serve with heavy cream or ice cream.

In my begging bowl

Violets and dandelions

jumbled together—

I offer them to the

Buddhas of the Three Worlds

—Ryokan, translated by Burton Watson

Hungry Ghost

Hungry ghosts appear on the Tibetan wheel of life as terrifying embodiments of endless craving. Beings with tiny mouths, long throats, and huge, unfillable bellies, practitioners of Buddhism commonly interpret these spirits as a metaphor for the ceaseless hunger and a craving endemic to the human condition. In the following passage, psychiatrist and Buddhist practitioner Mark Epstein investigates hungry ghosts as a model of the emotional longing and torment that he finds in his patients.

In searching through the Buddhist treasure house of myths and stories for guidance in working with emotional pain, I have returned again and again to the descriptions of the Hungry Ghost realm. For although the realm was originally described as another abode of sentient beings, distinct from the Human realm, it seems to embody many psychological qualities common to those of us in the West. As a patient of mine recently described it to me, she feels as if there is an anxious, insecure, and empty place at the center of her being that can never be touched by another person but that is desperate for contact. Every time she is disappointed, she reacts with a combination of unacknowledged rage and self-loathing, driving herself into a more and more alienated position. The *preta*, or hungry ghosts, perfectly describe this psychological predicament. Phantomlike creatures with withered limbs, grossly bloated bellies, and long, thin, narrow necks, the hungry ghosts in many ways represent a fusion of rage and desire. Tormented by unfulfilled cravings, insatiably demanding impossible satisfactions, the hungry ghosts are trying to fill a bottomless void within themselves. They are beings who have uncovered a terrible hollowness and who are desperate to erase that feeling. They cannot see that the damage has already occurred, that they must accept, not try to eradicate, their inner feelings. Their ghostlike state is representative of their attachment to the past.

In addition, these beings, while impossibly hungry and thirsty, cannot drink or eat without causing themselves terrible pain or indigestion. Their long, thin, narrow throats are so thin and raw that swallowing produces unbearable irritation. Their bloated bellies are in turn unable to digest nourishment; attempts at gratification only yield a more intense hunger and craving. Like my patient, these beings cannot take in a present-day, albeit transitory, satisfaction. It simply feels too insignificant. They remain obsessed with the fantasy of achieving complete release from the emptiness in their bellies and are stubbornly unaware that their desire is fantasy.

The hungry ghosts must come in contact with the ghostlike nature of their own longings in order to be free.

There is a well-known story in the Buddhist tradition, the story of Kisagotami, that illustrates the Buddha's approach to the plight of the hungry ghosts. Kisagotami was a young woman of the Buddha's time whose first child died suddenly just as he had learned to walk by himself, probably somewhere around his first birthday. Desperate in her love for the child, Kisagotami went from house to house in her village clasping the dead child to her breast asking for medicine to revive him. Most of her neighbors shrank from the sight of her and called her mad, but one man, seeing her inability to accept the reality of her son's death, directed her to the Buddha by promising her that only he had the medicine that she sought. Kisagotami went to the Buddha and pleaded with him for medicine. "I know of some," he promised. "But I will need a handful of mustard seed." As Kisagotami rose to find him some, however, he continued, "But I require some mustard seed from a house where no child, husband, parent, or servant has died."

Slowly, Kisagotami came to see that hers was not a unique predicament. She put the body of her child down in the forest and returned to the Buddha. "I have not brought the mustard seed," she told him. "The people of the village told me, 'The living are few, but the dead are many.'" The Buddha replied, in words that are said to have evoked a glimpse of Nirvana, "You thought that you alone had lost a son; the law of death is that among all living creatures there is no permanence." Some time later, as Kisagotami was attending her daily tasks, she noticed the lights of the village shining brightly one minute and then going out. "My state is like those lamps," she reflected, and the Buddha is said to have sent her a vision of himself saying the following words, "All living beings resemble the flame of these lamps, one moment lighted, the next extinguished; those only who have arrived at Nirvana are at rest."

Kisagotami's story resonates, not just because of our immediate sympathy for the horror of losing a child or because of our fear of a world in which such a tragedy is possible, but because we would all like to be freed from our angers, doubts, and insecurities. We were all injured, let down, and we all developed rage and bitterness as a result. Unable to accept the intensity of our own responses, we then attribute our own aggression to those who disappoint us and become even more alienated from those whom we also need. We all fear that aggression will prove more powerful than love. This is the predicament of the hungry ghosts as well. Kisagotami's story resonates because we are all, like her, yearning for nourishment that will undo the traumas of our past. In so doing, we continue to operate in a way that is driven by a childish fear of being overwhelmed by our own aggression. Deep down, we all feel that our situation is unique, that our unresolved emotional pain requires relief. In the privacy of our own minds, we are aggrieved and single-mindedly self-centered. We are still operating from a place that seeks absolute gratification, that is intolerant of frustration. Our own pleasure or unpleasure is our only reference point.

The most difficult part of Kisagotami's story for me comes when she lays her child down in the forest. Even though he has been dead for a long time, I still feel slightly aghast at the idea of her leaving him there. Yet this is precisely what the Buddha is asking us to do. He asks us to lay our long deceased child, our longing, down in the forest, the traditional site of intensive spiritual practice. The Buddha helped Kisagotami to find happiness not by bringing her dead child back to life, but by changing her view of herself.

This is precisely the task that faces the hungry ghosts and those of us who mirror their pain. The only nourishment that is capable of satiating the emptiness of the hungry ghosts is spiritual nourishment. Just as the hollowness of the hungry ghosts must be experienced in such a way that reparation is no longer sought from impossible sources, so the person afflicted with such feelings must make the hollowness itself the object of his or her meditation. Only then can pain or self-loathing be transformed into wisdom, a task in which both psychotherapy and meditation may well collaborate. The hungry ghosts are hungry for wisdom, but they get sidetracked by food. In a similar way, we can use our feelings of hollowness and insatiable longing to trick ourselves into discovering the truth of the Buddha's teachings. The hungry ghosts must learn to feed on their own emptiness before they can appreciate real food.

Light Vinegared Eggplant

This eggplant dish from abbess Soei Yoneda appears among the foods served at the Japanese hungry ghost offering feast, Obon (All Souls'), in August. It makes four small servings, according to the Japanese tradition, in which many dishes are served instead of one or two.

4 4-inch eggplants, caps removed

To make the sweet vinegar:
3 tablespoons rice vinegar
1½ tablespoons sugar
Pinch salt

Cut eggplants into fourths lengthwise. Cut each fourth crosswise into ⅛-inch slices.

In a medium saucepan, bring eggplant slices and ample water to a boil over high heat, reduce heat to medium, and simmer until cooked. The cooking time varies greatly, depending on the season and the eggplant.

Drain eggplant and cool to room temperature. Place cooled slices in a bowl and add sweet vinegar dressing. Toss until well coated.

May be served at room temperature or chilled, in separate small dishes or in one dish family style. Does not keep.

Vegetarian Chilli

This chilli can serve as a satisfying meal in itself when served with rice, or it can be used as a side dish.

2 medium onions, diced

4 cloves garlic, finely chopped

2 tablespoons oil

2 cups water

5 carrots, peeled and diced

5 celery stalks, diced

3 tablespoons chilli powder

2 green peppers, diced

2 cups corn kernels, canned or fresh

1 28-ounce can crushed tomatoes

1 cup cooked white beans (or canned)

1 cup cooked black beans (or canned)

Sauté onion and garlic in oil till soft but not brown. Add water, carrots, and celery, and cook till vegetables are nearly tender. Add remaining ingredients and bring to a boil. Simmer, stirring occasionally, for about 1 hour. Add a bit more water toward the end of the cooking time if chilli seems too thick.

This blessing is said at Zen monasteries when a grain of rice is offered to the hungry spirits before anyone takes a mouthful. This translation is by D. T. Suzuki.

O you of the spiritual worlds,

I now offer this to you;

Let this food fill the ten quarters

And all the spirits enjoy it.

Innocence

Innocence *and guilt* are two words that come up in connection
with the vegetarian debate. Here Buddhist practitioner John
McClellan suggests that no one is truly innocent; instead, he
claims that we all take life, whether we eat meat or whether we
abstain.

There would seem to be little justification for eating meat. There's no nutritional need, it's hard on the Earth, not that good for us, and the factory conditions in which we produce "animal products" are so appalling they beggar description.

But not eating meat might be playing things too safe. The function of all our actions as human beings should be to deepen awareness and arouse compassion for the liberation of all beings. But in my own experience, being a strict vegetarian seems to give rise to a subtle buffer between myself and the suffering world, shielding me from the very feelings I would most like to arouse.

Vegetarianism is so "karmically correct" it can isolate us from the experience of other beings, from those mindless ogres who *do* eat meat, and from the poor meat products themselves. It's a plea of innocence—"Myself *I* don't eat the stuff . . ." And I must confess that many of the other "Green" practices—such as recycling, Green voting, Green shopping, and money donations—give me the same feeling. You don't get off that easy.

Living in a society based on industrial-strength meat productions, we *know* what is happening to these animals. History holds no greater horrors than those we have created on our factory farms. Each one of us, through our passive and active acceptance of this, has a hand on the cage door, on the knife. Each of us is an accomplice. But every creature under heaven makes its living this same way, causing harm to others, and leaning on them for food, shelter, and recreation. All day long, creatures are bumping into other creatures, squashing them, killing and eating and drinking them, wearing and using them, walking and lying on them, destroying their homes. There is no personal boundary to this karmic responsibility—it radiates through every jewel in Indra's Net. A karmic debt "owed" by one is owed by all. Vegetarians owe as much as meat eaters, pacifists as much as fighters. There are no personal safe zones, no useful strategies for self-protection.

Therefore, rather than seeking only to avoid causing harm, which is impossible, perhaps we should also be asking ourselves: *What can one do with one's life* to offset this "karmic expense," to repay the debt of harm that inevitably accrues to our personal-universal account?

No one would begrudge the Buddha his private operating expenses, his robe (monocultured crops), bowl (forest products), daily rice (irrigated paddies), or the hecatomb of grasses, flowers, and insects crushed under his many lotus seats. Through his awareness and compassion, he took responsibility for his costs and redeemed them.

We might strive to do the same. We could use our precious and *expensive* (to others) human life to acknowledge and repay the grandmotherly kindness and the sacrifice of all beings who have willingly or unwillingly surrendered their lives or territory so that we may live.

When one is coming into a first awareness of the frightful suffering of our meat animals, being a vegetarian makes sense. Once this sensitivity is properly established, however, some might wish to resume eating meat—out of compassion—to take further painful responsibility for the suffering of all beings, to arouse broken heart and knowing mind.

Joshu Sasaki Roshi was sitting at the end of a long table all by himself toward the end of his eighty-first birthday party, watching the flies, when he suddenly snatched one out of the air and killed it—just for the sake of practice, for the precision, beauty, speed of it. This is the way he catches students; it is the practice of a Zen master, and he enjoys it. To a silent inquiry from a surprised student, he replied, "Die with the fly."

So, like this, die with your dish of meat, with everybody else's dish of meat. Embrace the death of all creatures as if it were your own, as though you were directly responsible for it, which you are. Die a thousand deaths with all sentient beings. Liberate them this way. Get bad broken heart forever for how we are forced to live. Cry whenever you see a well-fed North American.

In the Tibetan and American Indian traditions, meat is a sacrament: eating it is a gesture of sharing in the pain and pleasure of life, a way of taking responsibility for one's existence, bowing to the law of cause and effect, and an offering of compassion. There is, of course, no difference in principle between meat and vegetables in this regard. Dogen Zenji eats grains of rice with the same fearless mind. Willing to die with everything together.

So how do we turn this nice abstract theory into vivid personal experience, with the sharp edge of real practice? What you're looking for is a high ratio of awareness to consumption. Killing our food ourselves is of course best, but no one wants to do that anymore.

Try this: go visit a factory farm or slaughterhouse. Have a look at the animals on our farms. This is not the charming story we all remember from those Little Golden Books of the fifties, with red barns, grandpas with pipes, autumn foliage, and friendly animals. Has it become so bad that no one is allowed to even *look* anymore? All the more reason to go there yourself, in person. Be wary of trespassing charges, but be sure to meet your animal products face to face.

Talk to the animals in their cages. Hear their cries. Honor them; they greatly deserve it. Pray with them, for their lives, for your own life. They are dying so that we may live, suffering so that we may enjoy. What can we do with our lives to redeem this? All the buddhas will help us investigate this difficult situation.

For those who simply cannot bring themselves to eat meat—consider that vegetables are living beings too. Unlimited sympathy with sentient beings is the main point. Food is one of the things we use to arouse such a mind. Whatever one chooses to eat, abandoning hope or personal safety and accepting universal karma is a core practice. For particularly stubborn and intractable students, including serious vegetarians, this practice might require fresh, dead meat. There's nothing like it to tenderize tough heart.

A recipe poem by Gary Snyder.

How to Make Stew in the Pinacate Desert Recipe for Locke & Drum

A. J. Bayless market bent wire roller basket buy up parsnips, onion,
carrot, rutabaga and potato, bell green pepper,
& nine cuts of dark beef shank.
They run there on their legs, that makes meat tasty.

Seven at night in Tucson, get some bisquick for the dumplings.
Have some bacon. Go to Hadley's in the kitchen right beside the
frying steak—Diana on the phone—get a little plastic bag from
Drum—
Fill it up with tarragon and chili; four bay leaves; black pepper
corns and basil; powdered oregano, something free, maybe about
two teaspoon worth of salt.

Now down in Sonora, Pinacate country, build a fire of Ocotillo,
broken twigs and bits of ironwood, in an open ring of lava: rake
some coals aside (and if you're smart) to windward,
keep the other half ablaze for heat and light.
Set Drum's fourteen-inch dutch oven with three legs across the
embers.

Now put in the strips of bacon.
In another pan have all the vegetables cleaned up and peeled and
sliced.
Cut the beef shank meat up small and set the bone aside.
Throw in the beef shank meat,
And stir it while it fries hot,
lots of ash and sizzle—singe your brow—

Like Locke says almost burn it—then add water from the jeep
can—
add the little bag of herbs—cook it all five minutes more—and
then throw in the pan of all the rest.
Cover it up with big hot lid all heavy, sit and wait, or drink bud-
weiser beer.

And also mix the dumpling mix aside, some water in some
bisquick,
finally drop that off the spoon into the stew.
And let it cook ten minutes more
and lift the black pot off the fire
to set aside another good ten minutes,
Dish it up and eat it with a spoon, sitting on a poncho in the dark.

Red Cooked Beancurd and Cucumber

A *protein-rich vegan dish from Zen practitioner and cookbook author David Scott.*

1   medium cucumber, seeded, cut into strips 2" long and ¼" thick
    Salt
8   ounces beancurd, cut into 1" cubes
4   tablespoons vegetable oil (sesame seed oil, if available)
2   tablespoons soy sauce
1   red pepper, seeded, cut into strips 2" long and ¼" thick
2   teaspoons grated fresh gingerroot
4   tablespoons rice vinegar or cider vinegar
2   teaspoons sugar

Place the cucumber in a colander and sprinkle liberally with salt. Leave to stand for 20 minutes. Fry the beancurd in half the oil in a wok or frying pan and gently brown all sides of the cubes. Remove the beancurd from the pan and put into a bowl, sprinkle with the soy sauce, and leave to marinate. Rinse the cucumber under cold running water, drain, and pat dry on a tea towel. Add the remaining oil to the wok or pan and add the cucumber, red pepper, and ginger. Stir-fry over a high heat for 2–3 minutes. Transfer the contents of the pan to a serving dish. Add the vinegar, sugar, beancurd and soy sauce. Gently mix together and leave to marinate in the refrigerator for 4 or more hours. Refrigerated, it will keep for up to 3 days.

Steak Fajitas

Serves 4

3 medium onions, sliced

3 green peppers, sliced

3 tablespoons olive oil

1½ pounds boneless steak, thinly sliced

3 cloves garlic

1 jalapeño pepper, seeded and finely diced

½ cup chopped fresh cilantro

½ cup chopped tomato, fresh or canned

½ teaspoon salt

¼ teaspoon pepper

1 tablespoon lemon juice

8 soft flour tortillas

Sauté onions and peppers in oil over medium-high flame until just softening. Add steak slices and sear briefly. Turn heat to high, add other ingredients, and heat through. Serve in a bowl with warm tortillas.

You food, you animal plants
I take you, now, I make you wise
Beautiful and great with joy
Enlightenment for all sentient beings
All the hungry spirits, gods and buddhas who are sad
30:V:67
—Philip Whalen

Joshu's Bowls

Joshu was a renowned master of the T'ang period who is said to have attained enlightenment at the age of eighteen. He was mild-mannered and taught by gentle gestures rather than shouts. In this commentary on a koan originated by Joshu, known as "Joshu's Bowls," Koun Yamada Roshi examines everyday activities, such as eating, drinking, and cleaning up.

The Case: A monk asked Joshu in all earnestness, "I have just entered this monastery. I beg you, Master, please give me instructions!" Joshu asked, "Have you eaten your rice gruel yet?" The monk answered, "Yes, I have." Joshu said, "Then wash your bowls." The monk attained some realization.

Zen masters do not like abstract words or concepts such as *Buddha nature, enlightenment, nirvana,* and so forth. These terms are only instruments of explanation. But such terms do not actually touch the fact, still less can they grasp it. The verbal exchanges in Zen are, therefore, always concrete. In conceptual form, Joshu's questions would read, "Have you tasted *kensho* [enlightenment experience] yet?"

The monk's reply, "Yes, I have," means, "Yes, I am already enlightened." Joshu replies, "Then wash your bowls."

Through Zen one should become an ordinary person, a real person, not freakish, eccentric, or esoteric. So when Joshu told the monk that if he finished his meal he should wash his bowls, he meant if you have tasted *kensho* [enlightenment] wash away its glamour. At this the monk came to a deeper realization.

The other point of view from which this koan should be contemplated is that of the essential nature of the self, of being. As I repeatedly tell you, in the world of essence the logic of the absolute reigns. This means one thing is the whole, the whole is one thing. When you realize this world of essence, you will understand that you and the whole universe are one. When you stick up one finger, there is nothing but the finger in the whole universe. Just the finger. The finger and the whole universe are one. This is seeing in the absolute. This can be true because the finger, having no substance, is empty [of inherent self-existence]. This emptiness is nothing but the essential nature of the finger. The substance of all things is emptiness. The subject is empty, the object is empty. And the subject and object are one in emptiness from the very beginning. To ordinary common sense, subject and object oppose each other. There is you, seeing with your eyes, and there is the external object, seen by you. This is true not only of sight, but for all our senses. For the truly enlightened eye, however, this dualistic contrast is nothing but an illusion produced by one's thought. I do not know anything about Christianity, but I cannot believe that God created a dualistic world. The great enlightenment of Buddha tells us that there are no dualistic contrasts. When you stand up, you simply stand up, there is only standing up in the whole universe, and the substance of standing up is emptiness. Reflect for a moment on the mechanics of movies. What you see on the screen is a continuously flowing movie consisting of a multitude of single images being projected on the screen. Each image is projected for an instant and covers the entire screen. The movie is seen as a whole in the flowing continuity.

In the same way your life is the continuity of standing up, sitting down, laughing, sleeping, waking up, drinking, eating, and, of course, being born and dying. That is the continuity of the whole universe. Now, I presume you understand what Joshu means when he says, "Wash your bowls." I repeat, our life is nothing but the continuity of these actions, and they are nothing but the continuity of the whole universe.

A Recipe for Cleaning the Mind

Bernard Glassman Roshi writes that "Joshu's Bowls" is about the process of cleaning up, dropping the conditioning or attitude that keeps us separated from the next thing, starting afresh, and leaving no trace:

Just as we start cooking a meal by cleaning the kitchen, it's helpful to start the day by cleaning our mind. In Zen Buddhism, we clean the mind by the process of meditation, or zazen, which literally means "just sitting."

The basic ingredients are very simple:

> A space to meditate in.
> A cushion or chair on which to sit.
> And your body and mind.

Choose a time of day when your chances of being interrupted are minimal—early morning, before most people have gotten up, for example.

Find a space that is quiet, not too dark or too light, and where you are not likely to be disturbed. If necessary, close the door.

Make the space aesthetically pleasing. Depending on your taste, include an inspiring image, or a natural object such as a beautiful rock or flower. Candles and incense are optional as well.

Wear comfortable, non-binding clothes.

Assume a comfortable position. Back erect and without tension. Do not lean against the wall or the back of the chair.

Place your right hand palm up on your lap and left hand palm up on your right hand, thumbs slightly touching. This position is called the cosmic mudra and creates a restful environment for the mind.

If you are sitting on a chair, place your feet squarely on the ground with knees approximately six inches apart.

If you are sitting on a cushion (a folded blanket will also do nicely), adjust the height of the cushion so that both knees rest firmly on the ground. The equilateral triangle formed by this position gives support to both the back and spinal column.

Let your eyes remain half-closed, half-open, lightly resting on a spot on the floor approximately three feet in front of you. This will allow your eye muscles to relax while you keep an alert state of mind.

Place the tip of your tongue at the top of your palate, behind your top front teeth. As you inhale, count one. As you exhale, count two. Continue to ten and then repeat, from one to ten again.

As thoughts arise, let them come and go. Keep your attention on the counting. When you notice that thoughts have distracted you and you have lost your count—gently return to the counting. Start over at one.

Continue for a minimum of two and a maximum of thirty minutes.

Repeat daily—or at least once a week.

Apple Soufflé

In French, the word "souffle" means breath: a soufflé takes its name from the puff of wind, or breath, that elevates it. When making a soufflé, careful attention must be paid to make sure it doesn't collapse.

4 tablespoons unsalted butter

4 large cooking apples, peeled, cored, and sliced

¾ cup plus 1 tablespoon sugar

1 teaspoon cinnamon

4 tablespoons rum

4 egg yolks

⅓ cup flour

2 teaspoons cornstarch

1 cup plus 2 tablespoons milk

5 egg whites

Melt the butter in a heavy skillet over high heat. Add the apples and sauté for 3 minutes. Sprinkle ¼ cup plus 1 tablespoon sugar and the cinnamon and sauté until the apples are tender and the sugar is syrupy. Add 3 tablespoons of the rum; it will flame up, so be careful. Remove it from the heat immediately.

Butter a 2-quart soufflé dish and preheat the oven to 425°. Beat the egg yolks with the flour, cornstarch, and 2 tablespoons of milk.

Bring 1 cup of milk and ¼ cup sugar to a boil. Add a little of the hot milk to the yolk mixture and stir. Pour the yolks into the pot with the hot milk and return to the flame. Cook, stirring constantly and vigorously, until the mixture thickens and a bubble appears. Remove from heat, add the rest of the rum, and pour into a bowl.

Whip the egg whites until they are almost firm. Add the rest of the sugar and continue to beat until it is shiny. Fold the whites into the warm yolk mixture. Put the apples in the bottom of the soufflé dish. Top with the egg mixture. Bake 25 to 30 minutes until puffed and brown and firm on top. Serve immediately.

Floating Islands

This dessert, white puffs of meringue floating on a plate of custard, recalls the Zen admonition to "float like clouds, flow like water."

C u s t a r d

> 3 eggs
>
> ¼ cup brown sugar
>
> 2 cups scalded milk
>
> ⅛ teaspoon salt
>
> ½ teaspoon vanilla

Beat eggs lightly, combine ingredients except vanilla, and stir over double boiler about 7 minutes, or until mixture coats spoon. Chill. Flavor with vanilla.

M e r i n g u e

> 2 egg whites
>
> 4 tablespoons sugar
>
> ¼ teaspoon vanilla
>
> Pinch salt

Beat egg whites to soft peaks. Gradually beat in rest of ingredients. Bake in 425° preheated oven in muffin tins half filled with water. To serve, place custard in shallow bowl and lift meringues with spatula and float on custard. Top with slivered almonds, if desired.

How cold—

leek tips

washed white.

    —Basho, translated by Lucien Stryk

Karmapa

The Karmapa is the lineage holder of the Karma Kagyu, one of the five schools of Tibetan Buddhism. Helen Tworkov retells the story of an encounter between the late Karmapa (Rangjung Dorje, the Sixteenth Karmapa) and a young Western couple caught between two Eastern traditions.

The late Karmapa loved birds. Westerners called the regal guru the St. Francis of Tibet, for he was often seen at his monastery in Bhutan with birds perched on his shoulders or eating from his hand. Songbirds and birds of silence, those of brilliant plumage and dull-breasted females, carnivores and seed-eaters—all were welcome in his court.

Once I heard about a time during the mid-seventies when the Karmapa and his retinue were staying with some young American friends at the splendid Oberoi Hotel in New Delhi. Inspired by Baba Ram Das, Leo Heistein had quit his medical practice in California and he and his wife Susan had come to India to study with a secluded mountain yogi. But having met the Karmapa several years earlier and recognized the supremacy of his wisdom mind, they had courted his friendship and eagerly responded to his suggestion that they join him on his visit to Delhi. In his presence, they maintained the strict vegetarian diet of their Vedanta tradition, and would sometimes engage His Holiness in friendly debates about the different views of "self" expressed in the Brahmanic and Buddhist traditions.

One afternoon during their stay in Delhi, the Karmapa suggested that they visit the Jain hospital for birds in the old section of the city. A black Mercedes with a mango-turbaned chauffeur transported them through the dense maze of the Lajpat-Rai, the market that nestled into the shadows of the ancient Red Fort. The smell of dust filled the air and smoke twists rose from the dung fires that heated vats of oil-drenched take-away foods, which were handed to customers wrapped in sheets of newsprint. The driver yelled and waved his arms at the throngs of people, sacred cows, and laden ox-carts that jammed the narrow streets. From inside the Mercedes, they saw men walking naked, carrying nothing, their gaunt, dusty bodies drawing no attention, while women, holding deformed and blind babies up to the windows moaned "baksheesh, baksheesh." Everywhere puddles of yellow shit, and betel leaf spittle coughed up like blood, were ground into the dirt streets by fast-moving bare feet.

At the entrance to the red brick hospital, they were greeted by attendants swathed in white cotton and who, in keeping with the Jains' indiscriminate reverence for life, wore white gauze masks over their mouths to prevent the unwitting entrapment of invisible organisms.

They had barely passed the entryway when uncaged birds began to gather around the Karmapa. Some had little splints like toothpicks to help heal their broken bones, others hobbled with lame legs, and one female peacock had no legs at all. The Jains were very polite to the Tibetan holy man and gladly escorted him and his friends through the hospital.

As they inspected rows of crowded wire cages, His Holiness discoursed on the karmic order of birds. Songbirds came first. Pleasing to both eye and ear, these creatures were also virtuous in their feeding habits, eating only seeds, and through their droppings sowing flowers and fruit trees. Indeed, their habits, their diminutive beauty, and the tranquillity induced by their music merited their unequivocal place in the order of birds. But the bottom of the order offered no such clarity. Who should be the very last, wondered the Karmapa—birds of prey, or those scavengers that fed off carrion? Turkey vultures, for example, did not themselves kill, but offered none of the majestic grace of a hungry hawk nor the stunning aptitude of a trained falcon.

The Karmapa had laughed at this dilemma, and laughed, too, because he was happy to see so many birds diligently cared for by the kind Jains. It had been a fine afternoon, and upon driving back, His Holiness invited his American friends to dinner in the hotel's plush dining room.

A few hours later, after bathing and changing into fresh Indian clothing, Leo and Susan joined the Karmapa and his monks. Waiters in starched white cotton stood stiffly at attention near a rectangular banquet table that had been laid with a pink linen cloth, crystal glasses, gold-rimmed plates, and polished cutlery. The Karmapa had already taken the liberty of ordering a five-course feast.

This was not the India to which the American seekers had grown accustomed, but they welcomed this luxurious respite from their humble mountain retreat. Bolstered by this gracious setting and their convivial host, their conversation quickly became animated and lighthearted. The dining room began to fill, and across the floor, from a trio in tuxedos, came the familiar strains of Viennese waltzes.

Soon, the waiters placed two silver platters on either side of the table and proceeded to efficiently serve chunks of baked chicken smothered with a masala sauce. The Tibetans eagerly took up their forks, but Leo and Susan remained dumbfounded. The Karmapa said nothing and appeared to take no notice of the discomfort aroused in his American guests. Minutes later, two more platters arrived, this time with whole tiny roasted pheasants laid to rest on a bed of colored rice, their little eyes smaller than the fresh red tikka between Susan's brows. Leo could contain himself no longer. Making a sweeping gesture over the platters, he glared at the Karmapa and sputtered, "I just don't get it."

Undisturbed, the Karmapa continued eating, then smiled gently, shrugged, and quietly said, "It's a paradox."

Chicken Masala

Serves 4

3 tablespoons olive oil

2 pounds chicken parts (breasts or legs)

1 1" cube fresh ginger, chopped

5 cloves garlic, chopped

1 2"-long cinnamon stick

1 bay leaf

4 whole cardamom pods

2 whole cloves

2 dried hot peppers

1 teaspoon turmeric

5 tablespoons tomato sauce

5 tablespoons yogurt

1 tablespoon lemon juice

1 teaspoon salt

⅛ teaspoon pepper

Heat oil in large casserole-type pot and brown chicken well, a few pieces at a time. Remove chicken. Place ginger and garlic in blender with 2 tablespoons water and blend till smooth. Add mixture and next six spices to pot and stir over medium heat for 1 minute. Return chicken to pot. Mix tomato, yogurt, lemon, salt, and pepper, add to pot, and bring to boil. Simmer 1/2 hour, turning chicken occasionally. At end, raise heat and reduce sauce by half.

Mango and Apricot Chutney

1   large mango, peeled and chopped

4   apricots, peeled and chopped

1   medium onion, finely chopped

½   cup brown sugar

1   teaspoon fresh minced ginger

2   tablespoons apple cider vinegar

1   garlic clove, minced

½   cup raisins

½   teaspoon ground cumin

¼   teaspoon ground cloves

¼   teaspoon salt

1   jalapeño pepper, seeded and finely chopped

¼   teaspoon cinnamon

Combine all ingredients and simmer about 20 minutes. Let stand 15 minutes before serving.

Cucumber Raita

Serves 4 – 6

2 cups plain yogurt

1 medium cucumber, peeled and finely chopped

¾ teaspoon ground cumin

½ teaspoon salt

1 tablespoon chopped cilantro

Combine first 4 ingredients and chill well. Garnish with cilantro before serving.

"Kassapa, a practicer of self-mortification may do all these things [become a herb-eater, a millet-eater, a raw-rice eater, a wild-rice eater . . .] but if his morality, his heart, and his wisdom are not developed and brought to realization, then indeed he is still far from being an ascetic or a Brahmin. But, Kassapa, when a monk develops non-enmity, non-ill-will, and a heart full of loving-kindness, and, abandoning the corruptions, realizes and dwells in the uncorrupted deliverance of mind, the deliverance through his own wisdom, having realized it in this very life by his own insight, then, Kassapa, that monk is termed an asecetic and a Brahmin."

—Shakyamuni Buddha to his disciple Kassapa, as recorded in the Pali Canon, translated by Maurice Walshe

Last Meal

The Buddha's death was precipitated by a poisonous meal. The substance of his last meal—specifically, whether it contained contaminated pork or lethal mushrooms—has been a focus of the Buddhist vegetarian debate for centuries. Here, religion scholar Stuart Smithers examines the historical record and its attendant controversy.

What the historical Buddha ate for his last meal has been the subject of much debate. The controversial passage from the *Mahaparinibbana Sutta*, the sutta that recounts the Buddha's final days, tells us that on his last night, the Buddha rested in the home of Cunda, a metal smith apparently known to the Buddha. In honor of his guest, Cunda prepared (probably not personally) "hard and soft delicious food, and also a large quantity of *sukaramaddava*." The difficulty lies in the translation of *sukaramaddava*. The amateur mycologist Gordon Wasson studied the available literature on the problem and admirably summarized it in his essay, "The Last Meal of the Buddha."

> The first part of that compound word, *sukara-*, is simple: "pertaining to pig or swine," *suk*—being cognate with Latin *sus*. The second element is generally thought to mean tidbits, dainties, but whether as a specially delicate part of the pig's meat or as food of which swine were especially fond, whether a subjective or objective genitive, no one can say. Rhys Davids, noticing that in Bihar there was a common edible underground fungus, translated *sukaramaddava* by "truffles." This was a successful pitch, considering that by "truffles" he meant an underground fungus common thereabouts, although no truffle (*tuber*) has been discovered so far in Bihar."

Drawing on the available scholarship, Wasson builds a convincing case that *sukaramaddava*, while not a truffle, must have been a kind of *mushroom grown on a spot trodden by pigs*.

But even if Wasson is correct about the translation of the term, the mushrooms were only one item on the menu. What were the "hard and soft delicious foods"? "Soft food" is defined in the *Vinaya* (IV 92) [the earliest record of Buddhist monastic rules] as "the five [kinds of] meals; cooked rice, food made with flour, barley-meal, fish, meat." Here, too, we cannot say with certainty that meat was served as one of the "soft foods," but we can say that meat might have been, that there was no inherently Buddhist reason why it would not have been.

There are, of course, other indications in the canon that Buddha did eat meat. There is, for example, the account of a nun, Uppalavanna, who obtained meat from a cattle rustler and thereafter contributed the meat to the Buddha. When making the gesture, one of the Buddha's attendants, receiving the meat, said to Uppalavanna, "You, sister, have pleased the lord with this meat. . . ."

Perhaps the most definitive answer to the question is given by the Buddha in the *Vinaya* in the famous story of the attempt by his cousin, Devadatta, to wrest control of the sangha [the monastic community] by creating a schism based on an appeal for stricter rules and regulations. Devadatta proposed that monks should live only in forests and never visit towns, monks should only wear rags and never accept donated robes, monks should not accept invitations to meals, they should live only "at the foot of a tree" and not in dwellings of any sort, and monks should never eat fish or meat. The Buddha responded to Devadatta by saying that whoever wished to live according to those rules could do so (except that a dwelling was required during the monsoon season), but that to do so was voluntary and not required.

Although the Buddha did not make a prohibition against eating meat, there were certain conditions that pertained to the eating of meat. According to the *Vinaya*, meat—or any food—could be eaten so long as the monk did not know that the food had been specially and specifically killed for the purpose of feeding the sangha. But what is easily overlooked is that the Buddha made special conditions for the procurement and consumption of *all* food. This institution of begging for one's meal meant that despite one's likes and dislikes, one ate whatever was given, whether it was meat or nuts, tasteless or delicious, stale or fresh. Another incident in the *Vinaya* (IV 82) reminds us that the Buddha intended his disciples to struggle with the unconscious habits of appetite: if you are satisfied, do not eat again later just because some tempting dish has been put in front of you.

The canonical material does not support a prohibition against meat eating. A vegetarian who delights in his or her own meal, who eats too much, who rejects what is offered, who is unconsciously driven by habitual appetites and hunger, is undoubtedly more "at fault" (according to the Buddha of the *Vinaya*) than someone who eats meat because it is served to him or her. What the Buddha seemed to be most interested in was the *attitude* one had toward food and eating. The conditions that the Buddha applied to food and eating might allow us to discover the actual *force* of our hunger and how this force, when we are unconscious of it, keeps us from awakening.

A second look at restrictions on eating in Buddhism makes clear that the essential issues are not ethical or moral, but rather conditions for further discipline, practice, and questioning. The mysteries of food, desire, and hunger are central to all religious disciplines, but in the canonical texts of early Buddhism, we can see the extraordinary concerns taken by the Buddha to call attention to this very direct experience of seeing into one's true nature.

Cashew Rice

Serves 6

This recipe from the Kopan monastery in Nepal, which uses some of the same ingredients as the five foodstuffs, was adapted by Betty Jung.

⅓ cup vegetable oil

2 cups red onion

1 cup fresh or frozen peas

½ carrot, shredded

1 cup raisins, presoaked in water

1½ cups cashew nuts

6 cups long-grain white rice, steamed

Salt to taste

Heat the oil in a wok over medium to medium-high heat. Add 1 cup of the onion and deep-fry until crispy. Remove onion and set aside. Repeat with the remaining onion. Pour off excess oil, leaving 2 tablespoons in wok. Add peas, carrots, raisins, and cashew nuts. Stir-fry 1–2 minutes. Remove from heat. Add stir-fried mixture and crispy deep-fried onions to freshly steamed rice. Toss. Salt to taste. Serve hot.

Hearty Stew with Seasoned Dumplings

Serves 6

In *Tibet, they eat their meat inside dumplings. In the West, we usually let our dumplings float on top of stews and other meat dishes.*

Stew ingredients

2 pounds beef suitable for stewing, cut into 1½" cubes

Flour for dredging

2 teaspoons salt

Freshly ground black pepper to taste (about ¼ teaspoon)

3 tablespoons fat or vegetable oil

4 onions, peeled and chopped

6 carrots, peeled and cut in half

1 pound parsnips, peeled and cut into chunks

1 clove garlic, crushed

1 bay leaf

2 cups beef broth, red cooking wine, beer or water

1 tablespoon flat Italian parsley, minced

Dumpling mixture

1 cup flour

1½ teaspoons baking powder

½ teaspoon salt

½ teaspoon dried thyme

½ teaspoon dried sage

2 tablespoons shortening

½ cup milk

Add half of the salt and a few grinds of pepper to the flour; dredge the beef in the seasoned flour mixture; then brown several pieces at a time, in the fat or oil in a heavy pot over high heat; remove to a plate. Add the chopped onion and let cook until golden, stirring occasionally so it doesn't burn; remove to the plate. Drain the fat; return the beef and onion to the pot. Add all the remaining ingredients except the parsley. Cover and simmer for 1½ to 2 hours or until the meat is tender. (The recipe can be made ahead of time up to this point; it tastes best if refrigerated for a day.)

About 20 minutes before serving, prepare the dumpling mixture by mixing the first five ingredients together; cut in the shortening until mixture starts to crumb. Add all of the milk and mix lightly. Drop the dumpling mixture by rounded tablespoonfuls on top of stew, when just simmering. Simmer for 10 minutes; cover and simmer 10 minutes more. Taste and add remaining salt and pepper as needed. Sprinkle with parsley and serve.

[I BURN UP THE DEER IN MY BODY]

I burn up the deer in my body.
I burn up the tree in my stove.

I seldom let a carrot go to seed, and I
grind up every kind of grain.

How can I be and never be an
inconvenience to others, here,

where only the Vulture is absolutely pure

and in the Chicago River
are carp?
—Lew Welch

Middle Way

Zen teacher Kosho Uchiyama Roshi explains how preparing food is
not a rehearsal for the meal to come but a complete activity in
itself. This commentary on Zen master Dogen's Instructions to
the Tenzo (head cook) reveals how cooking gruel tonight for
tomorrow's breakfast is an embodiment of the Middle Way.

In Buddhism, the view which only sees living in the world as impermanent and our trying to accumulate anything as useless is referred to as *danken*, whereas a way of life which assumes that things must be accumulated and is based solely on setting up the limited goals of wealth, good health, or offspring, is called *joken*. Both of these views, *danken* and *joken*, are understood to be one-sided. This understanding brought about the exposition of the Middle Way.

Middle Way does not mean halfway. Nor does it mean some sort of watered-down, defeated compromise or shallow eclecticism. Rather, Middle Way means to accept this contradiction of impermanence and cause and effect within your own life. To accept this contradiction means to forbear and overcome it without trying to resolve it. At its very essence life is contradiction, and the flexibility to forbear and assimilate contradiction without being beaten down by it nor attempting to resolve it *is* our life force.

To express this concretely in terms of our daily attitude, it means to live without projecting goals while yet having a direction. Since everything is impermanent, there is no way of telling what might happen to us in the next instant—we could very well die! To set up a goal of purpose is to invite disappointment by seeing things move in a direction contrary to these goals. Yet, we are certainly in trouble if we decide that since we have no future goals or expectations there is no present direction. The *Tenzo Kyokun* (*Instructions to the Tenzo*) teaches that we must prepare for the next morning the night before. "Next, all the officers meet in the kitchen or pantry and decide what food is to be prepared for the following day, for example, the type of rice gruel, the vegetables, the seasoning. . . ."

In this seemingly matter-of-course passage there is an extremely vital teaching to be found. In this world of impermanence, we have no idea of what may occur during the night. . . . Nevertheless, we are told to prepare the gruel for the following morning and make a plan for lunch. Moreover, we are to do this as *tonight's work*. In preparing the meal for the following day as tonight's work, there is no goal for tomorrow being established. Yet, our direction for right now is clear: prepare tomorrow's gruel. Here is where our awakening to the impermanence of all things becomes manifest, while at the same time our activity manifests our recognition of the law of cause and effect. In this routine matter of preparing tomorrow's gruel as this evening's work lies the key to the attitude necessary for coping with the absolute contradiction of impermanence and cause and effect.

Much too often we go about our lives holding on to some future goal without thinking about our present direction, or about the direction of our lives as a whole. When we stop projecting goals and hopes in the future, and refuse to be led around by them, yet work to clarify our lives, that is the *direction* of the present, then we will discover an alive and dynamic practice. At the juncture of this contradiction we will begin to understand the function of the tenzo.

Swiss Muesli

Serves 4

Swiss farmers traditionally soak their breakfast muesli the night before and add fresh fruit in the morning.

1½ cups oat flakes

½ cup wheat flakes

½ cup bran

⅓ cup wheat germ

⅓ cup raisins

⅓ cup chopped dried dates

⅓ cup chopped dried apricots

2 tablespoons walnuts

Milk to cover

Grapes, grated apple, peaches, or other fresh fruit

Mix dry ingredients in bowl and add milk to cover. Soak overnight. Serve with fresh fruit.

Green Pea Soup with Mint

Serves 4 – 6

4 tablespoons butter

1 onion, minced

2 pounds shelled peas (or small frozen)

1 teaspoon salt

1 teaspoon sugar

3 cups chicken stock (or vegetable stock, if
   vegetarian)

1 bunch fresh mint leaves

   Light cream or crème fraîche, optional garnish

6 fresh mint leaves (garnish)

Melt the butter in a heavy pan and add the onion. Sauté until transparent; add peas and chopped mint. Allow to cook for 5 minutes over low heat. Bring to the boil and simmer for about 8 minutes. Blend in a food processor or blender and then pass the mixture through a fine mesh strainer to remove any pea skins. Refrigerate overnight, to let the flavor develop. When ready to serve, reheat the soup until it's very hot, almost boiling. Serve in warmed bowls. Garnish with a swirl of cream and a mint leaf.

BLESSING

And when the cook is finished, the meal can be offered and blessed.
Monk Michael Roach explains that this Tibetan food blessing is "a
well-known grace that reflects the wish to reach enlightenment for
the good of every living being."

In faith I offer this delectable food

Of a thousand flavors, cooked to perfection,

To the Victors and their sons and daughters;

By this act may every living being

Revel in the richest feast

Of perfect meditation.

Nature

Zen temple cooking, known as Shojin, *affirms a connection to nature by responding to the season and the situation with subtlety and grace. This style of cooking appreciates whatever food is available in season, and prepares it in such a way as to cool someone who is warm or warm someone who is cool. The word Shojin is composed of the characters meaning spirit and progress; in addition to making one more sensitive to the natural world, it is also a discipline meant to improve one's training through the preparation and consumption of only the simplest (vegetarian) foods. Abbess Soei Yoneda, who trained in this rigorous discipline of Shojin cooking for more than seventy years, reflects on this practice.*

P reparing food is training for the spirit, and taking care to make food as delicious and beautifully arranged as possible cultivates our aesthetic sensitivity. There is no more splendid form of training.

It is in the kitchen where this work is carried out. When the kitchen is kept clean, fresh, and easy to work in, the vegetables, sea plants, and other ingredients, chosen according to the season, take on added luster. We must always keep in mind, though, that no matter how far the world progresses, these ingredients remain the blessings of nature. We must also be aware that natural disaster and want can occur at any moment. It is vitally important to be prepared for such calamities by eliminating waste and pursuing with humility and respect the "spirit of the kitchen." Nor should we abandon a culinary project when we have forgotten one of the ingredients. A sensitivity toward how to make the best of what is on hand will allow unexpected success. And the happiness of cooks when this happens is something only they can know.

Furthermore, use the pots and pans you are used to. Surrounded by familiar kitchen implements, the cook is like a symphony conductor, ready to draw forth beautiful music from the instruments at his fingertips. . . .

Though our modern lives are full of comfort, we have gradually become distant from our natural environment. Living in homes with heaters and air conditioners isolates us from the changes in the four seasons. We tend to forget the gentle breeze in the tree tops and the warm rays of the sun. *Shojin* cooking emphasizes rather than hides the delights of the seasons and seasonal changes. As the world progresses, this ideal becomes more and more difficult to realize. But *shojin* cooking melts into nature. On a cold and snowy day in winter, one sits hunched over, warming the tips of one's fingers on a Steamed Savory Cup. And in the summer's heat there are cold noodles (somen) on a bed of ice and deep green leaves. Or one can enjoy cold, white tofu as it floats in clear water.

Pine Cones

The portions for the following recipe by Soei Yoneda are small, since a Japanese meal usually involves many small dishes rather than one or two large ones. This dish was designed to be served in the autumn and will yield four servings.

Before the commuter train station was completed about 10 minutes' walk from the Sanko-in, the temple area was as quiet and isolated as Tibet. At that time, in autumn one could hear odd popping sounds coming from some parts of the temple grounds. The little cones of the red pines had dried and were opening up percussively. In this event was born an idea for this dish. The ingredients are just tofu and shiitake mushrooms, and the result is amazingly delicious. The commuter train made the area a convenient place to live, so houses and apartments surround the temple today. The quiet that allows one to hear pine cones popping open is part of the past.

1 cake regular tofu
3 large dried shiitake mushrooms, reconstituted in
   tepid water, stems cut off, and chopped fine

For flavoring shiitake:

1 teaspoon vegetable oil
2 teaspoons soy sauce
½ teaspoon sugar
   Vegetable oil for deep-frying

Ginger-Soy Sauce

  1 part fresh ginger juice

  2 parts soy sauce

Place tofu in a medium-sized saucepan with water to cover. Bring to a boil over medium heat and simmer 1 minute. Drain. Wrap tofu in a clean kitchen towel, place on cutting board, and weight with about 1 pound for 45 minutes.

Pour 1 teaspoon vegetable oil in small pan. Add chopped shiitake mushrooms and stir-fry about 30 seconds. Add the soy sauce and sugar and stir-fry until liquid is absorbed—about 1 minute.

Place pressed tofu in a bowl and mash with your hand, leaving some small lumps. Add flavored shiitake mushroom and mix gently by hand.

Heat oil to medium temperature (340°) over medium heat.

Form tofu-shiitake mixture into 12 small pine-cone shapes about 1½"–2" long and weighing about 1 ounce each. Deep-fry until golden brown. Drain on rack or absorbent paper.

Mix ginger-soy sauce. Eat hot! Dip one side into ginger-soy sauce before serving, or serve it as a dip accompanying the pine cones. Serve in individual dishes or family style on one plate. Decorate the serving with pine needles.

A Sanko-in Recipe for Ginger Tempura

Fresh ginger acts as an appetizer, freshens the palate, and also warms the body. It is especially good as an hors d'oeuvre or served between the courses of a heavy meal.

3 ounces fresh ginger, peeled

3 tablespoons flour

⅙ teaspoon salt

3 tablespoons water

  Vegetable oil for deep-frying

  Salt

Cut ginger into medium-thin rounds across the fiber grain, then cut rounds into fine julienne strips.

  Mix flour, salt, and water well to make a batter. Place ginger in batter and toss to coat well.

  Heat oil to medium temperature (340°) and deep-fry ginger in 4 portions. Drain and sprinkle with salt. Serve hot. Does not keep.

BLESSING

Serving Food:

In this food
I see clearly
the presence of the entire universe
supporting my existence.

Looking at the plate filled with food:

All living beings
are struggling for life.
May they all have
enough food to eat today.

Just before eating:

The plate is filled with food.
I am aware that each morsel is
the fruit of much hard work
by those who produced it.

—Thich Nhat Hanh

Oryoki

Oryoki can refer to the Buddha's eating bowls or to formal Zen eating practice, an essential part of monastic life and meditation retreats. To practice oryoki, participants eat from three or four (depending on tradition) bowls set in a nest, tied together with a cloth. It begins with a series of drum rolls and prayers; the meal is then served and consumed as part of a precisely articulated ritual, which leaves no waste and no dishes to clean. Here Zen master

Taizan Maezumi Roshi comments on the meal gathas, *or blessings, said throughout the eating ceremony.*

I n the *Fukushu Hampo* ("Rules for Eating Meals"), Dogen Zenji says "the dharma is the meal, and the meal is the Dharma. The Meal *Gathas* are about how we share the meal as the Dharma. I vividly remember Reirin Yamada Roshi (former chief abbot of Eiheiji) telling me, when I was studying with him at Zenshuji, "If you really understand the Meal *Gathas*, all the Buddha's teaching is there." At that time, I didn't quite understand what he meant. Maybe I still don't. But at least I do understand a little more than I did then, and I agree with him. More and more, I find the meal *gathas* a wonderful way of appreciating life.

We call the opening verse *gyohatsu*—opening the bowls. *Gyo* means practice, action, deed. *Hatsu* means bowl. *Gyohatsu*, therefore, means practice-bowl, or using the bowl to eat, to have a meal. The written character *gyo* in Chinese is considered a synonym of "the Way": "practice" is "the Way." The shape of the character *gyo* suggests a person lifting up both legs, which means walking. The character *gyo* also indicates a corner or a cross-road—a "way." Thus, the words "walking" and "way" have etymologically the same expression and implication. Practice, itself, is the Way. Walking, itself, is the Way. Acting, itself, is the Way. I see a very fascinating wisdom of no-division in that. Altogether, they are one. Without a path, you definitely can't walk anywhere. The two are not separate things. Eating food and preparing food, together, form a unity. Only in such a unity is there real peace.

We start [the blessing] by reciting the four major aspects of Buddha's life: Buddha was born, and enlightened, and taught, and entered nirvana. [See pp. 132–33 for blessing text.] In Zen, we also describe *hasso jodo*, eight aspects of *jodo* (accomplishment of the Way). First, descending or coming down from *tosotsu* heaven (the fourth heaven in the realm of desires, in Indian cosmology). Second, being conceived. Third, being born. Fourth, becoming a monk. Fifth, defeating the demons or evils. Sixth, attainment, accomplishment. Seventh, turning the dharma wheel. Eighth, nirvana. Each time we eat, we reflect upon these at the very beginning.

Even reflecting only upon this opening verse, if you really understand it, everything is there. Each moment, we are being conceived. "Being conceived" means to start living, to have life. Dogen Zenji says that the gravest matter of the Buddha Dharma is to clarify life and death. When you seriously think about it, perhaps most of us would be ashamed of how little we know about ourselves—our life, our death.

What is our life really? Before this life, where was I? This life can't just appear. In a way, your birth is given to you by your parents and yet it's not. Parents can't give us life. Our life is not a thing that belongs to them or that they can control. It's totally out of their control. How many people in the world want to have babies but can't? On the other hand, many don't want children, yet it happens. It's not the parents' choice to give life or not. That is to say, our life has its own life beyond what we may think or feel about it. That's what those, such as Dogen Zenji, who have deep religious insight say.

After the aspects of Buddha's life, the first verse of the *gathas* continues with "Now I open Buddha Tathagata's eating bowls." They are *oryoki*, Tathagata's eating bowls—not just something made of wood or clay, but Buddha's eating bowls. *O* means to respond, to be equal to, or to be adequate; *ryo* means amount; and *ki* is the container. So *oryoki* is the container which holds the appropriate amount. Who eats from the Buddha's eating bowls?

Later on, the *gatha* reads that we eat to maintain this body to practice. But there is more to it than that. We take food not only to nourish the body, but more importantly to nourish the mind. What is the best food for the mind? Needless to say, it's the Dharma. And, as I mentioned above, food and the Dharma are the same thing. In a way, we are eating "ourselves" in order to maintain ourselves. In other words, we appreciate oryoki, carrying the right amount of Dharma, as the life of Shakyamuni Buddha, which is our life.

"In the midst of the Three Treasures with all sentient beings, let us recite the names of Buddha." In Japanese, this line also carries the connotation that we penetrate, or gaze at the Three Treasures. Through the Three Treasures, we ask to be confirmed as one with the names of Buddha which follow. Then we recite the names of Buddha as the names of the Three Treasures. The names of the Buddha: from Dharmakaya Vairochana Buddha through future Maitreya Buddha and all Buddhas in the ten directions. The names of the Dharma: Mahayana Sadharma Pundarika Sutra, and Maha Prajna Paramita. And the names of the Sangha: all Bodhisattvas and Mahasattvas.

Two more verses follow before eating. The first of these, which begins with "First, seventy-two labors brought us this food," contemplates the meal itself, relating it to our practice. This line refers to the seventy-two positions in the traditional organization of a monastery, with hundreds of monks in residence, to be self-sufficient. These positions include not only farming, harvesting, and cooking, but also all the work needed to keep the monastery functioning. Thus are the meals made possible. Recognizing each and all the seventy-two labors implies appreciating each other in the monastic Sangha, and the nature of the harmony which makes the Sangha function as "One Body." In the modern context, the "seventy-two labors" symbolizes the innumerable steps which made it possible for the meal to be in this particular bowl. Recognizing the Sangha of all sentient beings, we recognize the "One Body" as one's self.

Continuing, the verse reminds us ". . . we should know how it comes to us," and ". . . we should consider whether our virtue and practice deserve it." In this way, the verse aims at further improvement and refinement in contemplating the meal as an aspect of one's own practice.

The next verse, which begins with "First, this food is for the Three Treasures," focuses on one's practice in relation to others. We contemplate being together to accomplish the Buddha Way. Reciting, "We eat this food with everyone," we recognize self and other as One in the Three Wheels. Each one of the Three Wheels (giver, receiver, and things given) are equally *kujaku*: peace in nirvana, peace in emptiness. In oryoki, the Three Wheels are the meal, the one who provides it and the one who eats it. The giver is also the receiver; the receiver is also the giver. The same applies to the things given and received. This life, contained in oryoki, is the life of the Three Treasures giving, receiving, and sharing. In this way, we maintain our life as the Dharma carrier. Our life is already in complete realization as we are in accordance with the wisdom and compassion of the Three Treasures. Opening the oryoki, receiving, giving, and appreciating are equally the very life of the Buddha.

This verse also reflects upon our practice as manifesting the Three Pure *Kai* (precepts): "We eat to stop all evil, to practice good, to save all sentient beings . . ." Finally, our vow "to accomplish the Buddha Way together" brings us back to the first verse on the aspects of Buddha's accomplishment of the Way.

Dogen Zenji says: "All the Buddhas of past, present, and future will become Shakyamuni Buddha, at the attainment of their Buddhahood." Elsewhere, he says Shakyamuni Buddha is "this very mind is the Buddha." In other words, realization or enlightened life is not just the life of someone else who lived someplace else sometime ago. It is the life of each of us at this very moment. That's what I interpret as opening the Tathagata's eating bowls. We eat not only to nourish this particular body, but to be in peace with all beings.

Savory Cornbread

*O*ryoki can be practiced with any kind of food. Professional chef and Zen student Ed Rothfarb offers this recipe.

"I first had a version of this cornbread at the Zen Center of Los Angeles during a sesshin. Served for breakfast, its aroma preceded it into the hall, and its moist texture and savory taste was so satisfying that I inquired about the recipe. Through the generosity of the tenzo I was able to get the basic idea for this dish and later served my version of it at the Sagaponack, New York, Zendo for the second meal during a retreat."

1	tablespoon oil for the pan
6	cups yellow cornmeal
1½	cups unbleached white flour
1½	cups whole wheat flour
12	teaspoons baking powder
2	teaspoons salt
2	teaspoons dried sage
1	teaspoon dried oregano
12	teaspoons unsulfured molasses
12	eggs, large
2	cups buttermilk
4½	cups cream-style corn (15-ounce cans)
1½	cups corn oil
1½	cups green onions, green part only, sliced thin
2	cups red peppers, chopped fine
3	cups corn kernels (fresh or frozen)
4	cups sharp Cheddar, grated

Oil a large metal baking pan (14" x 14" x 2") and heat in pre-heated 350° oven for 10 minutes.

In a large bowl, mix the next 5 ingredients. In a separate large bowl mix second 5 ingredients. Combine the 2 in a large bowl, but do not overmix. Add remaining ingredients. Bake for 1 hour, the first 25 minutes on the lower oven shelf, then transfer to the top shelf for the remaining 35 minutes. Bake until golden brown and a skewer inserted into middle comes out dry.

Black Bean and Roasted Pepper Salad

S e r v e s   6 – 8

Spicy and flavorful, this salad would go well with the cornbread recipe on p. 128.

4 green peppers

4 red peppers

2 cups dry black beans, soaked overnight and drained

6 cups water

¼ cup olive oil

   Fresh lime juice, to taste

2 ripe tomatoes, peeled and chopped

Dressing

1 teaspoon lime juice

1 tablespoon white wine vinegar

1 teaspoon crushed coriander seeds

2 tablespoons chopped fresh cilantro

1 garlic clove, chopped fine

1 teaspoon salt

¼ teaspoon black pepper

2 jalapeño peppers, seeded and diced

¼ cup light olive oil

Preheat the oven to 350°. Place peppers on a large shallow baking dish and bake for 1 hour, checking every 20 minutes or so to turn. The skins should become brown but the peppers should not burn. After an hour, remove the peppers to a plate and let cool; when cool enough to handle, remove the skins from the peppers by rubbing them lightly in your hands. Seed the peppers; cut the roasted peppers into thin strips and set aside.

Rinse the soaked beans in cold running water and drain again. Place beans in a large heavy pot and cover with the 6 cups of water and oil; bring to a boil. Simmer about 25 minutes, stirring occasionally, until the beans are tender but not too soft. Drain.

While the beans are cooking prepare the dressing by combining all of the ingredients except the oil; whisk in the oil last. When beans are finished toss in the dressing. Marinate for 1 hour at room temperature. Taste the beans, add lime juice as needed. Mix in the roasted peppers and fresh tomatoes and serve.

This meal blessing is recited at the Zen Center of Los Angeles during the opening of the oryoki bowls and the serving of the food.

Buddha was born at Kapilavastu
Enlightened at Magadha
Taught in Varanasi
Entered Nirvana at Kusinagara
Now I open Buddha Tathagata's eating bowls
May we be relieved from self-clinging with all sentient
    beings.

In the midst of the three treasures
With all sentient beings
Let us recite the names of Buddha.

Pure Dharmakaya Vairochana Buddha
Complete Sambhogakaya Vairochana Buddha
Numerous Nirmanakaya Shakyamuni Buddhas
Future Maitreya Buddha
All Buddhas throughout space and time
Mahayana Saddharma Pundarika Sutra
Great Manjusri Bodhisattva
Mahayana Samatabhadra Bodhisattva
Great compassionate Avalokitesvara Bodhisattva
All Bodhisattva Mahasattvas
Maha Prajna Paramita.

This food comes from the efforts of all sentient beings, past and present, and its ten advantages give us physical and spiritual well-being and promote pure practice.

We offer this meal of three virtues and six tastes to the Buddha, Dharma, and Sangha, and to all the life in the Dharma worlds.

First, seventy-two labors brought us this food; we should know how it comes to us.
Second, as we receive this offering, we should consider whether our virtue and practice deserve it.
Third, as we desire the natural order of mind to be free from clinging, we must be free from greed.
Fourth, to support our life, we take this food.
Fifth, to attain our Way we take this food.

All those of the spiritual worlds, now I give you this offering. This food will pervade everywhere.

First, this food is for the Three Treasures.
Second, it is for our teachers, parents, nation, and all sentient beings.
Third, it is for all beings in the six worlds.
Thus we eat this food with everyone,
We eat to stop all evil,
To practice good,
To save all sentient beings,
And to accomplish our Buddha Way.

Preparation

Thirteenth-century Zen master Dogen's eloquent and profound "Instructions to the Tenzo (head monastery cook)" teaches that preparing food is a Buddha activity, a spiritual practice. A great reformer, Dogen brought the focus of Buddhist practice back to daily life: among his many writings, his instructions on cooking, reprinted here, are the best known. This text, lengthy and complex, is known not as a "cookbook" but as a book on how to *cook your life. This version of Dogen's text was translated by Kazuaki Tanahashi and Arnold Kotler.*

Instructions to the Cook

Z en monasteries have traditionally had six officers who are all Buddha's disciples and all share buddha activities. Among them, the tenzo [chief cook] is responsible for preparing meals for the monks. *Regulations for Zen Monasteries* states, "In order to make reverential offerings to monks, there is a position called tenzo."

Since ancient times this position has been held by accomplished monks who have way-seeking mind, or by senior disciples with an aspiration for enlightenment. This is so because the position requires wholehearted practice. Those without way-seeking mind will not have good results, in spite of their efforts. *Regulations for Zen Monasteries* states, "Use your way-seeking mind carefully to vary the menus from time to time, and offer the great assembly ease and comfort." Long ago, Guishan Lingyou, Dongshan Shouchu, and other great teachers held this position. A tenzo is not the same as an ordinary cook or waiter.

During my stay in Song China, in spare moments I questioned senior monks who had held various positions, and they spoke to me from their experience. Their words are the bones and marrow of the buddha ancestors who have attained the way and have been passed on since olden times. We need to read *Regulations for Zen Monasteries* carefully to understand the tenzo's responsibilities, and then consider carefully the words of these senior monks.

The cycle of the tenzo's work begins after the noon meal. First go to the director and assistant director to receive the ingredients for the next day's morning and noon meals—rice, vegetables, and so on. After you have received these materials, take care of them as your own eyes. Zen Master Baoning Renyong said, "Protect the property of the monastery; it is your eyeball."

Respect the food as though it were for the emperor. Take the same care for all food, raw or cooked.

Next, in the kitchen, the officers carefully discuss the next day's meal, considering the tastes, the choice of vegetables, and the kinds of rice-gruel. *Regulations for Zen Monasteries* states, "The officers who oversee the kitchen should first discuss the menu-planning for the morning and noon meals." These officers are the director, assistant director, treasurer, *ino* [overseer of ceremony], tenzo, and work leader. Soon after the menu is decided, post it on the boards in front of the abbot's room and the study hall. Then prepare the gruel for the next morning.

When you wash the rice and prepare vegetables, you must do it with your own hands, and with your own eyes, making sincere effort. Do not be idle even for a moment. Do not be careful about one thing and careless about another. Do not give away your opportunity even if it is merely a drop in the ocean of merit; do not fail to place even a single particle of earth at the summit of the mountain of wholesome deeds.

Regulations for Zen Monasteries states, "If the six tastes [bitter, sour, sweet, hot, salty and plain], are not suitable and if the food lacks the three virtues [mildness, cleanliness, formality], the tenzo's offering to the assembly is not complete." Watch for sand when you examine the rice. Watch for rice when you throw away the sand. If you look carefully with your mind undistracted, naturally the three virtues will be fulfilled and the six tastes will be complete.

Xuefeng was once tenzo at the monastery of Dongshan Liangjue. One day when Xuefeng was washing rice, master Dongshan asked him, "Do you wash the sand away from the rice or the rice away from the sand?"

Xuefeng replied, "I wash both sand and rice away at the same time."

"What will the assembly eat?" said Dongshan. Xuefeng covered the washing bowl.

Dongshan said, "You will probably meet a true person some day."

This is how senior disciples with way-seeking mind practiced in olden times. How can we of later generations neglect this practice? A teacher in the past said, "For a tenzo, working with the sleeves tied back is the activity of way-seeking mind."

Personally examine the rice and sand so that rice is not thrown away as sand. *Regulations for Zen Monasteries* states, "In preparing food, the tenzo should personally look at it to see that it is thoroughly clean." Do not waste rice when pouring away the rice water. Since olden times a bag has been used to strain the rice water. When the proper amount of rice and water is put into an iron pot, guard it with attention so that rats do not touch it or people who are curious do not look in at it.

After you cook the vegetables for the morning meal, before preparing the rice and soup for the noon meal, assemble the rice buckets and other utensils, and make sure they are thoroughly clean. Put what is suited to a high place in a high place, and what belongs in a low place in a low place. Those things that are in a high place will be settled there; those that are suited to be in a low place will be settled there. Select chopsticks, spoons, and other utensils with equal care, examine them with sincerity, and handle them skillfully.

After that, work on the food for the next day's meals. If you find any grain or weevils in the rice, remove them. Pick out lentils, bran, sand, and pebbles carefully. While you are preparing the rice and vegetables in this way, your assistant should chant a sutra for the guardian spirit of the hearth.

When preparing the vegetables and the soup ingredients to be cooked, do not discuss the quantity or quality of these materials which have been obtained from the monastery officers; just prepare them with sincerity. Most of all you should avoid getting upset or complaining about the quantity of the food materials. You should practice in such a way that things come and abide in your mind, and your mind returns and abides in things, all through the day and night.

Organize the ingredients for the morning meal before midnight, and start cooking after midnight. After the morning meal, clean the pots for boiling rice and making soup for the next meal. As tenzo you should not be away from the sink when the rice for the noon meal is being washed. Watch closely with clear eyes; do not waste even one grain. Wash it in the proper way, put it in pots, make a fire, and boil it. As ancient master said, "When you boil rice, know that the water is your own life." Put the boiled rice into bamboo baskets or wooden buckets, and then set them onto trays. While the rice is boiling, cook the vegetables and soup. You should personally supervise the rice and soup being cooked. When you need utensils, ask the assistant, other helpers, or the oven attendant to get them. Recently in some large monasteries positions like the rice cook or soup cook have been created but this should be the work of the tenzo. There was not a rice cook or a soup cook in olden days; the tenzo was completely responsible for all cooking.

When you prepare food, do not see with ordinary eyes and do not think with ordinary mind. Take up a blade of grass and construct a treasure king's land; enter into a particle of dust and turn the great dharma wheel. Do not arouse disdainful mind when you prepare a broth of wild grasses; do not arouse joyful mind when you prepare a fine cream soup. Where there is no discrimination, how can there be distaste? Thus, do not be careless even when you work with poor materials, and sustain your efforts even when you have excellent materials. Never change your attitude according to the materials. If you do, it is like varying your truth when speaking with different people; then you are not a practitioner of the way.

If you encourage yourself with complete sincerity, you will want to exceed monks of old in wholeheartedness and ancient practitioners in thoroughness. The way for you to attain this is by trying to make a fine cream soup for three cents in the same way that monks of old could make a broth of wild grasses for that little. It is difficult because the present and olden times differ as greatly as the distance between heaven and earth; no one now can be compared with those of ancient times. However, if you practice thoroughly there will be a way to surpass them. If this is not yet clear to you it is because your thoughts run around like a wild horse and your feelings jump about like a monkey in the forest. When the monkey and horse step back and reflect upon themselves, freedom from all discrimination is realized naturally.

This is the way to turn things while being turned by things. Keep yourself harmonious and wholehearted in this way and do not lose one eye, or two eyes. Taking up a green vegetable, turn it into a sixteen-foot golden body; take a sixteen-foot golden body and turn it into a green vegetable leaf. This is a miraculous transformation—a work of buddha that benefits sentient beings.

When the food has been cooked, examine it, then carefully study the place where it should go and set it there. You should not miss even one activity from morning to evening. Each time the drum is hit or the bell struck, follow the assembly in the monastic schedule of morning zazen [sitting meditation] and evening practice instruction.

When you return to the kitchen, you should shut your eyes and count the number of monks who are present in the monks' hall. Also count the number of monks who are in their own quarters, in the infirmary, in the aged monks' quarters, in the entry hall, or out for the day, and then everyone else in the monastery. You must count them carefully. If you have the slightest question, ask the officers, the heads of the various halls or their assistants, or the head monk.

When this is settled, calculate the quantities of food you will need: for those who need one full serving of rice, plan for that much; for those who need half, plan for that much. In the same manner you can also plan for a serving of one-third, one-fourth, one-half, or two halves. In this way, serving a half portion to each of two people is the same as serving one average person. Or if you plan to serve nine-tenths of one portion, you should notice how much is not prepared; or if you keep nine-tenths, how much is prepared.

When the assembly eats even one grain of rice from Luling, they will feel the monk Guishan in the tenzo, and when the tenzo serves a grain of this delicious rice, he will see Guishan's water buffalo in the heart of the assembly. The water buffalo swallows Guishan, and Guishan herds the water buffalo. [Here Dogen refers to monk Guishan who predicted he would be reborn as a water buffalo with the words "I am a monk of Guishan" written on his side. He told his disciples, "When you call me the monk of Guishan, I will be a water buffalo. When you call me a water buffalo, I will be a monk of Guishan. Then how are you going to call me?]

Have you measured correctly or not? Have the others you consulted counted correctly or not? You should review this closely and clarify it, directing the kitchen according to the situation. This kind of practice—effort after effort, day after day—should never be neglected.

When a donor visits the monastery and makes a contribution for the noon meal, discuss this donation with the other officers. This is the traditional way of Zen monasteries. In the same manner, you should discuss how to share all offerings. Do not assume another person's functions or neglect your own duties.

When you have cooked the noon meal or morning meal according to the regulations, put the food on trays, put on your kashaya [patched robe worn over one shoulder by a monk], spread your bowing cloth, face the direction of the monks' hall, offer incense, and do nine full bows. When the bows are completed, begin sending out the food.

Prepare the meals day and night in this way without

wasting time. If there is sincerity in your cooking and associated activities, whatever you do will be an act of nourishing the sacred body. This is also the way of ease and joy for the great assembly.

Although we have been studying Buddha's teaching in Japan for a long time, no one has yet recorded or taught about the regulations for preparing food for the monks' community, not to mention the nine bows facing the monks' hall, which people in this country have not even dreamed of. People in our country regard the cooking in monasteries as no more developed than the manners of animals and birds. If this were so it would be quite regrettable. How can this be?

During my stay at Mt. Tiantong, a priest named Yong from Qingyuan Prefecture held the position of tenzo. One day after the noon meal when I was walking along the eastern covered walkway to a sub-temple called Chaoran Hut, he was in front of the buddha hall drying some mushrooms in the sun. He had a bamboo stick in his hand and no hat on his head. The sun was very hot, scorching the pavement. It looked very painful; his backbone was bent like a bow and his eyebrows were as white as a crane.

I went up to the tenzo and asked, "How long have you been a monk?"

"Sixty-eight years," he replied.

"Why don't you let a helper do it?"

"Others are not myself."

"Reverend Sir, you follow regulations exactly, but as the sun is so hot why do you work so hard this?"

"Until when should I wait?"

So I stopped talking. As I was walking further along the covered walkway, I thought about how important the tenzo's position is.

In the fifth month of the sixteenth year of Jiading [1223], I was staying on a ship at Quingyuan. One time, while I was talking with the captain, a monk about sixty years old came on board. He talked to a Japanese merchant and then bought some mushrooms from Japan. I invited him to have tea and asked where he came from. He was the tenzo of Mt. Ayuwang.

"I am from Shu in western China," he said, "and have been away from my native place for forty years. Now I am sixty-one years old. I have visited monasteries in various places. Some years ago, priest Daoquan became abbot of Guyun Temple at Mt. Ayuwang, so I went to Mt. Ayuwang and entered the community. I wanted to make a noodle soup, but we did not have mushrooms, so I made a special trip here to get some mushrooms to offer to the monks from the ten directions."

I asked him, "When did you leave there?"

"After the noon meal."

"How far away is Mt. Ayuwang?"

"Thirty-four or thirty-five li [about twelve miles]."

"When are you going back to your monastery?"

"I will go back as soon as I have bought mushrooms."

I said, "Today we met unexpectedly and had a conversation on this ship. Is it not a good causal relationship? Please let me offer you a meal, Reverend Tenzo."

"It is not possible. If I don't oversee tomorrow's offering, it will not be good."

"Is there not someone else in the monastery who understands cooking? Even if one tenzo is missing, will something be lacking?"

"I have taken this position in my old age. This is the fulfillment of many years of practice. How can I delegate my responsibility to others? Besides, I did not ask for permission to stay out."

I again asked the tenzo, "Honorable Tenzo, why don't you concentrate on zazen practice and on the study of the ancient masters' words rather than troubling yourself by holding the position of tenzo and just working? Is there anything good about it?"

The tenzo laughed a lot and replied, "Good man from a foreign country, you do not yet understand practice or know the meaning of the words of the ancient masters."

Hearing him respond this way, I suddenly felt ashamed and surprised, so I asked him, "What are words? What is practice?"

The tenzo said, "If you penetrate this question, how can you fail to become a person of understanding?"

But I did not understand. Then the tenzo said, "If you do not understand this, please come and see me at Mt. Ayuwang sometime. We will discuss the meaning of words." He spoke in this way, and then he stood up and said, "The sun will soon be down. I must hurry." And he left.

In the seventh month of the same year, I was staying at Mt. Tiantong when the tenzo of Ayuwang came to see me and said, "After the summer practice period is over, I am going to retire as tenzo and return to my native place. I heard from a fellow monk that you were staying here, so I thought I should come to see you."

I was moved with joy. I served him tea and we talked. When I referred to the discussion of words and practice which had taken place on the ship, the tenzo said, "To study words you must know the origin of words. To endeavor in practice you must know the origin of practice."

I asked, "What are words?"

The tenzo said, "One, two, three, four, five."

I asked again, "What is practice?"

"Nothing in the entire universe is hidden."

We talked about many other things, which I will not introduce now. If I know a little about words or understand practice, it is because of the great help of the tenzo. I told my late master Myozen about this in detail and he was extremely pleased.

I later found a verse which Xuedou wrote for a monk:

Through one word, or seven words, or three times five, even
if you thoroughly investigate myriad forms
nothing can be depended upon.
Night advances, the moon glows and falls into the ocean.
The black dragon jewel you have been searching for is
  everywhere.

What the tenzo had told me corresponded with Xuedou's
poem. So I knew all the more that the tenzo was truly a person
of the way.

   By studying this poem we know that the words we saw
before were one, two, three, four, five; the words we see now
are six, seven, eight, nine, ten. Fellow monks of later generations, from this you should understand practice and from that
you should understand words. If you make effort in this way,
you will understand pure one-taste Zen beyond words. If you
do not make such an effort, you will be troubled with the poison of five-taste Zen [Zen classified along ordinary lines: ordinary peoples', Mahayana, etc.]. Then you will not be able to
prepare the monks' food properly.

We can hear ancient stories and see present examples of
monks in the position of tenzo. Much has been written and ex-
plained about this. It is the heart of the practice of the way.

   Even if you become the abbot of a monastery, you
should have this same mind. *Regulations for Zen Monasteries*
states, "Prepare both meals of the day attentively and plenti-
fully. Make certain that the four types of offering [food,
clothes, bedding, and medicine] are not lacking, just as the
World-honored One offered his descendants the gift of the
twenty remaining years of his life. [The Buddha died at 80 instead of living to 100.] The merit of the light from even the
smallest portion of the white hair tuft between his eyes [one
of the marks of the awakened one] is inexhaustible." In this
regard, it also states, "Just think about how best to serve the
assembly, and do not worry about limitations. If you have un-

limited mind, you will have limitless happiness." This is the way the abbot attentively serves the assembly.

In the art of cooking, the essential consideration is to have a deeply sincere and respectful mind regardless of the fineness or coarseness of the materials. Isn't it so, that by offering to the Tathagata [the Buddha] a bowl of water with which she had washed rice, a woman obtained inconceivable merit throughout her various lives? By offering half a mango to a monastery, King Ashoka [a Buddhist king in India] created wholesome roots as the last act of his life. As a result, he received from Buddha prediction of attaining the way and realized the great fruit. Even a large offering to Buddha, if insincere, is not as good as a small one which is sincere. This is the right practice for people.

A refined cream soup is not necessarily better than a broth of wild grasses. When you gather and prepare wild grasses, make it into a fine cream soup with your true mind, sincere mind, and pure mind. This is because when you serve the assembly—the undefiled ocean of buddha-dharma you do not notice the taste of fine cream or the taste of wild grasses. The great ocean has only one taste. How much more so when you bring forth the buds of the way and nourish the sacred body. Fine cream and wild grasses are equal and not two. There is an ancient saying that monks' mouths are like a furnace. You should be aware of this. Know that even wild grasses can nourish the sacred body and bring forth the buds of the way. Do not regard them as low or take this lightly. A guiding master of humans and devas should be able to benefit others with wild grasses.

Again, do not consider the merits or faults of the monks in the community, and do not consider whether they are old or young. If you cannot even know what categories you fall into, how can you know about others? If you judge others from your own limited point of view, how can you avoid being mistaken? Although the seniors and those who came after differ in appearance, all members of the community are equal. Furthermore, those who had shortcomings yesterday can act correctly today. Who can know what is sacred and what is ordinary? *Regulations for Zen Monasteries* states, "A monk whether ordinary or sacred can pass freely through the ten directions."

If you have the spirit of "not dwelling in the realm of right and wrong," how can this not be the practice of directly entering unsurpassable wisdom? However, if you do not have this spirit, you will miss it even though you are facing it. The bones-and-marrow of the ancient masters is to be found in this kind of effort. The monks who will hold the position of tenzo in the future can attain the bones-and-marrow only by making such an effort. How can the rules of revered ancestor Baizhang [initiator of monastic regulations in China] be in vain?

After I came back to Japan I stayed for a few years at Kennin Monastery, where they had the tenzo's position but did not understand its meaning. Although they used the name tenzo, those who held this position did not have the proper spirit. They did not even know that this is a buddha's practice, so how could they endeavor in the way? Indeed it is a pity that they have not met a real master and are passing time in vain, violating the practice of the way. When I saw the monk who held the tenzo's position in Kennin Monastery, he did not personally manage all of the preparations for the morning and noon meals. He used an ignorant, insensitive servant, and he had him do everything—both the important and the unimportant tasks. He never checked whether the servant's work was done correctly or not, as though it would be shameful or inappropriate to do so—like watching a woman living next door. He stayed in his own room, where he would lie down, chat, read sutras, or chant. For days and months he did not come close to a pan, buy cooking equipment, or think about menus. How could he have known that these are buddha activities? Furthermore, he would not even have dreamed of nine bows before sending the meals out. When it comes time to train a young monk, he still will not know anything. How regrettable it is that he is a man without way-seeking mind and that he has not met someone who has the virtue of the way. It is just like returning empty-handed after entering a treasure mountain or coming back unadorned after reaching the ocean of jewels.

Even if you have not aroused the thought of enlightenment, if you have seen a person manifesting original self, you can still practice and attain the way. Or if you have not seen a person manifesting original self, but have deeply aroused the aspiration for enlightenment, you can be one with the way. If you lack both of these, how can you receive even the slightest benefit?

When you see those who hold positions as officers and staff in the monasteries of Great Song China, although they serve for a one-year term, each of them abides by three guidelines, practicing these in every moment, following them at every opportunity: (1) Benefit others—this simultaneously benefits yourself. (2) Contribute to the growth and elevation of the monastery. (3) Emulate masters of old, following and respecting their excellent examples.

You should understand that there are foolish people who do not take care of themselves because they do not take care of others, and there are wise people who care for others just as they care for themselves.

A teacher of old said:

Two-thirds of your life has passed,
not polishing even a spot of your sacredness.
You devour your life, your days are busy with this and that.
If you don't turn around at my shout, what can I do?

You should know that if you have not met a true master, you will be swept away by human desire. What a pity! It is like the foolish son of the wealthy man who carries a treasure from his father's house and discards it like dung. You should not waste your time as that man did.

People of the way who held this position in the past kept equally high standards of responsibility and virtue. Great Guishan had his awakening as tenzo. Dongshan Shouchu said, "Three jin [about one and half pounds] of hemp," [Dongshan's awakening] when he was tenzo.

If anything should be revered, it is enlightenment. If any time should be honored, it is the time of enlightenment. When you long for enlightenment and follow it taking sand and offering it to Buddha is beneficial; drawing a figure of a Buddha and paying homage also has an effect. How much more so to be in the position of tenzo. If you act in harmony with the minds and actions of our ancient predecessors, how can you fail to bring forth their virtue and practice?

In performing your duties along with the other officers and staff, you should maintain a joyful mind, kind mind, and great mind.

"Joyful mind" is the mind that rejoices. You should think: "If I were born in the realm of gods, I would be attached to pleasure and would not arouse the aspiration for enlightenment nor have the opportunity to practice. Then how could I cook food to offer to the three treasures?" The most excellent of all things are the three treasures. Even Indra's virtue cannot be compared to them, nor can that of a wheel-turning king.

Regulations for Zen Monasteries states, "Respected in the world, quiet and secluded from daily affairs, pure and unconditioned—these qualities belong most of all to the community of monks." We are fortunate to be born in the human realm and even beyond this we have the good fortune of cooking meals to be offered to the three treasures. Is this not a great causal relationship? We should be most grateful for this.

You should also think, "If I were born in hell, in the realm of hungry ghosts, beasts, or demons, or if I were born in the eight difficult situations I could not with my own hands cook pure meals to offer to the three treasures, even if I were to use a monk's miraculous power. This is so because it would be my destiny to be a vessel of suffering, with body and mind bound up."

But since you are cooking pure meals in this lifetime, this is a life of rejoicing and a body of rejoicing. It is a wholesome cause from limitless eons, it is merit that does not erode. I hope you will do your work and cook the meal this very day, at this very moment, with this body, the fruit of myriad births and thousands of lifetimes, thereby creating merit for myriad beings. To penetrate this is joyful mind. Even if you become a wheel-turning king, there will be no more merit if the meal you cook is not an offering to the three treasures; your effort will be like bubbles or vanishing flames.

"Kind mind" is parental mind. Just as parents care for their children, you should bear in mind the three treasures. Even poor or suffering people raise their children with deep love. Their hearts cannot be understood by others. This can be known only when you become a father or a mother. They do not care whether they themselves are poor or rich; their only concern is that their children will grow up. They pay no attention to whether they themselves are cold or hot, but cover their children to protect them from the cold or shield them from the hot sun. This is extreme kindness. Only those who have aroused this mind can know it, and only those who practice this mind can understand it. Therefore, you should look after water and grain with compassionate care, as though tending your own children.

The great master Shakyamuni Buddha gave the final twenty years of his life to protect us in this age of the decline of learning. What was his intention? He offered his parental mind to us, without expecting any result or gain.

"Great mind" is a mind like a great mountain or a great

ocean. It does not have any partiality or exclusivity. You should not regard a pound as light or a ton as heavy. Do not be attracted by the sounds of spring or take pleasure in seeing a spring garden. When you see autumn colors, do not be partial to them. You should allow the four seasons to advance in one viewing, and see an ounce and a pound with an equal eye. In this way, you should study and understand the meaning of *great*.

If the tenzo of Mt. Jia had not studied the word *great*, he would not have awakened senior Fu by laughing at him. If Zen master Guishan had not understood the word *great*, he would not have blown the unlit firewood three times. If priest Dongshan had not known the word *great*, he would not have taught a monk by saying, "Three jin of hemp." You should know that these great masters all studied the word *great* over hundreds of matters. This they brought forth the great shout of freedom, expounded the great principle, penetrated the great question, trained a great student, and in this way completed the single great matter.

The abbot, officers, staff, and other monks should never forget about these three kinds of mind.

In the spring of the third year of Katei [1237], this was written for the students of later generations who will study the way, by Dogen, dharma transmitting monk, abbot of Kannondori Kosho Horin Zen Monastery.

Citrus Salad with Bitter Greens

A recipe from Annie Sommerville, Executive Chef at Greens restaurant, which is operated by members of the San Francisco Zen Center:

1 handful of escarole hearts

1 small head of radicchio

1 handful of watercress or frisée hearts or a mixture of the two

   Citrus Vinaigrette (recipe follows)

2 or 3 kumquats, thinly sliced and seeded

2 naval or blood oranges

2 tangerines

1 ruby grapefruit

Remove the outer leaves of the escarole, using only the tender, light green inner leaves; cut or tear them into large pieces. Trim the base of the radicchio, carefully separate the leaves, and cut or tear them. Sort through the watercress and pluck the small sprigs, discarding the long stems and bruised leaves. Wash and dry the greens in a spinner; wrap loosely in a damp towel and refrigerate until needed.

Make the vinaigrette, then toss the kumquats in a little of it to soften their acidity.

Using a sharp knife, remove the peel and white pith from the fruit, slicing a piece off the top and bottom, then working down the sides. Be sure to remove all of the outer white membrane. Slice the oranges and tangerines into rounds; slice the grapefruit in half lengthwise, then into half-moons. Remove all seeds.

Place the greens in a bowl and toss with half of the vinaigrette. Arrange them on a platter or individual plates and place the fruit on top, alternating the slices. Sprinkle the kumquats over the salad and drizzle with the remaining vinaigrette.

Citrus Vinaigrette

½ teaspoon minced orange zest

2 tablespoons fresh orange juice or 1 tablespoon each orange and tangerine juice

1 tablespoon champagne vinegar

¼ teaspoon salt

3 tablespoons light olive oil

Combine everything but the oil in a small bowl, then whisk in the oil. Makes about ⅓ cup.

Beet Salad with Watercress

A recipe by Edward Espe Brown, former tenzo at Tassajara Mountain Zen Center.

5–6 large or 10–12 smaller beets, about 1 pound

1 bunch watercress

2 green onions

¼ cup balsamic vinegar

3 tablespoons honey

¾ teaspoon allspice

Salt

Black pepper

1 tablespoon olive oil

Baking the beets will give them a richer flavor. Leave an inch of stems on the beets and place them whole in a baking dish. Add about ½ inch of water. Cover and bake in a 375° oven for 45–60 minutes. Remove and let cool, then slip off the stems and skin by hand. Slice the beets. Remove any tough stems, then wash and dry the watercress. Slice the green onion thin. Save some of the green onion for garnish, then mince the rest of the slices, especially the white part.

Combine the vinegar and honey. Use about ⅔ of it to dress the beets, with the minced green onion. Then season the beets with the allspice, salt, and pepper.

Toss the cress with the olive oil, then with the remaining vinegar-honey mixture and some salt and pepper.

Serve the beets and cress side by side; garnish beets with green onion slices.

MAKING SALAD

after Eihei Dogen

I rub the dark hollow of the bowl
with garlic, near to the fire enough
so that fire reflects on the wood,
a reverie that holds emptiness
in high regard. I enter the complete
absence of any indicative event,
following the swirl of the grain,
following zero formal and immanent
in the wood, bringing right to
the surface of the bowl the nothing
out of which nothing springs.

I turn open the window above the sink
and see fire, reflected on the glass,
spring and catch on a branch a light
wind tosses about. Here or there,
between new leaves the Pleiades,
like jewels in the pleromatic lotus,
flash. I watch the leaves swirl
and part, gathering light fresh
from Gemini, ten millennia away, fresh
from Sirius—holding each burning
leaf, each jewel within whatever light
a speck of conscious mind can make,
unshadowed by reflection or design,

impartial. Out the tap, from a source
three hundred feet down, so close
I feel the shudder in the earth, water
spills over my hands, over the scallions
still bound in a bunch from the store.
I had thought to make salad, each element
cut to precision, tossed at random
in the turning bowl. Now I lay the knife
aside. I consider the scallions. I consider
the invisible field. Emptiness is bound
to bloom—the whole earth, a single flower.
—Margaret Gibson

Qualities

Lama Yeshe, a Tibetan Buddhist monk, suggests that the naming of an object—such as a nectarine—encourages us to "overestimate its qualities" and endows it with a false reality. By approaching things without relying on labels, we have a better chance of appreciating them as they are.

B uddhism believes that all human beings have the ability to understand our own true nature, and that developing such understanding is the most important thing we can do. All the problems, confusion, and dissatisfaction we experience are the result of not having developed this understanding, and until we do, we shall never be free from bondage. The main human problem is not understanding our own reality.

Therefore, all the teachings of the Buddha, no matter which you choose, are directed at helping us realize both the conventional nature of our lives and universal totality, or sunyata [the lack of independent self-existence]. Both are of great importance.

As our mind perceives these conventional existences, it tries to identify the reality of what it sees, to comprehend the reality of our own existence, others' existence, universal existence, the existence of all phenomena. And how do we end up? By naming perceived objects in an attempt to give them reality.

Something is there—a nectarine, for example—and what we try to do is identify its reality. So we give it the name "nectarine" to represent its reality. As a matter of fact, the true reality of the nectarine is just the collection of its constantly moving parts: the right elements have gathered, the fruit has developed organically, and it's somehow ready to eat. Apart from this superficial interdependence and moment-to-moment transformation of the elements that constitute the nectarine, you can't add further dimensions to its existence; to do so is to exaggerate, or what I call overestimate, its qualities.

When we understand the cooperative, interdependent mode of existence of the nectarine, its transitory energy, its color and vibration, and also the relationship between ourselves and the nectarine, we will begin to understand its universal reality—or at the least, we will have the potential to do so soon. . . .

We pick something up, touch it, look at it closely, and

finally declare, "Ah, here's a good one [nectarine]." But by the time we get home, it's rotten. Now, the question is—we've labeled a particular substance "nectarine"—but what is the reality of that substance. Is a rotten nectarine a nectarine?

Calling something a nectarine is supposed to somehow touch its reality, but from a Buddhist point of view this is a very superficial exercise. The superficial mind labels something a nectarine, and a nectarine comes into existence. But in our delusion, we hear the word nectarine and a concrete nectarine enters our perception. But there's no such thing as a concrete nectarine—inherently existent, independent, permanent. Fundamentally, the relationship between the name nectarine and the reality of the nectarine is the product of ignorance, developed through our not having touched the nectarine's reality.

Instead of thinking of a nectarine as a nectarine, try calling it "John"! Give it a human name!

Lama Yeshe offers a short meditation:

Think as follows. Two or three hundred years ago, none of the mentally labeled objects that we find today in supermarkets existed. Then, people started intellectualizing, and superstitious fantasies grew. Then, they produced Coca-Cola and all the other supermarket things with which we're so familiar. All these things have been labeled, or produced, by the mind of superstition. From their own side, these objects have no trace of duality or self-existence. As long as you want to see things dualistically, the dual appearance is there. When you see totality, dualistic appearances vanish. You and I are one totality of non-duality. Be aware of totality; feel totality. Totality has no idea of good or bad, beautiful or ugly. Now meditate on totality with intensive awareness.

Nectarine Chutney

½ cup brown sugar

1 pound fresh nectarines, pitted and chopped

1 teaspoon apple cider vinegar

1 clove garlic, chopped

¼ cup chopped onion

1 teaspoon grated ginger

¼ teaspoon ground cinnamon

3 pinches ground mace

3 pinches cayenne pepper

¼ teaspoon salt

Combine sugar and nectarines and simmer until sugar is melted. Add remaining ingredients and cook about 15 minutes over medium heat till fruit is tender. Cool and allow to sit for an hour or 2. Serve same day.

Chicken Breasts with Nectarines

Serves 4

2 whole chicken breasts, split in half
  Salt and pepper
¼ teaspoon cinnamon
2 tablespoons butter
½ cup chicken broth
½ cup red wine
4 nectarines, chopped

Sprinkle chicken with salt, pepper, and cinnamon. Melt butter in large frying pan and add breasts, turning till well browned. Add broth, wine, and nectarines, and simmer, covered, for about 20 minutes. Remove breasts to a warm platter. Reduce sauce by half over high heat. Pour over breasts.

POEM

Nineteenth-century Zen monk and poet Ryokan wrote this poem on receiving a gift of seven pomegranate seeds.

Splitting them, eating
picking them apart, eating
breaking into them, eating—
after that never
letting them out of my mouth
—translation by Burton Watson

Receiving

The oldest Buddhist food-related ritual is the monastic alms round,
in which monks and nuns receive and eat whatever they are freely
given. Following is a story of novice Zen monks from Donald
Richie.

D uring the Meiji era the acolytes of a certain temple in Osaka were embarrassed to beg. Begging, however, was a part of their training.

They were to stand at street corners and bow, their baskets held out. Or, they were to remain in front of a shop and chant until they were given something. Or, they were to ring a small bell and walk slowly through the streets, soliciting from the passers-by.

This embarrassed the acolytes. They giggled and nudged each other. Or, they became red in the face and grew timid. Or, they sat down and refused altogether.

The deacon took them to task. He pointed out that begging was perfectly honorable. It has been a part of priestly training since the old days in China. It was good for the mind. All acolytes everywhere had begged. But this advice had no effect. He added that the roshi would not approve of their attitude. This too had no effect.

In due time the roshi heard about the embarrassed acolytes. One by one he called them in and asked why priests begged. The answers were various. It humbled the spirit. Or, it was another way of meditating. Or, it made one properly grateful. Nonetheless, they agreed, begging continued to embarrass them.

The roshi decided to give a lecture on the subject:

"One ought to beg because of the sheer difficulty of it. Even in the old days, when there was not enough food, begging was difficult. Now that there is enough to eat and there are telegraph poles and steam engines, it is even more difficult.

"I understand your concern. It is for your dignity. You feel that begging lacks dignity. Dignity lies in difficulty. It is, for example, much more difficult to receive than it is to give. Anyone can give, and most would if the gift were small enough. But receiving something, particularly something small, is very difficult. It is so difficult, begging, that one ought be proud rather than ashamed.

"I mention dignity because you are still young and are consequently troubled by such empty concerns. And since you apparently desire this worthless quality, I will give it to you. To have dignity you must have need. I will give you this need."

The acolytes, pleased, gazed at each other. They were to receive something. The roshi continued:

"You will receive this from me in the spirit in which I intend it. I will bestow upon you a very real need. Through it you will attain a dignity, and because of it you will cast dignity away. I give you a true necessity."

He then went to the temple kitchen and told those there to prepare no more food.

After that the acolytes, hungry and thin, took to begging with an earnestness they had not known before. Their stomachs so growled that they forgot about both embarrassment and dignity. They stood on the street corners and bowed. They chanted in front of shops until rewarded. They walked through the streets ringing their small bells. This they did with their whole beings, with never a thought of anything else.

This had continued for a time. The acolytes were not only thinner, they were more serious. The roshi called them together:

"When one extreme has been reached, it is then necessary to reach another. This has all been useless, quite without point. It has been a waste. But I think that now you better understand. Food will be served. Begging will be continued."

There were no questions. The acolytes had understood.

The Dalai Lama's Momos

S e r v e s   4

These momos, or dumplings, are a traditional Tibetan favorite. This recipe comes from Tenzin Gyatso, His Holiness the Fourteenth Dalai Lama.

F o r   t h e   F i l l i n g

  1 pound potatoes

  3 tablespoons olive oil

  6 onions, chopped

12 ounces mushrooms, chopped

12 ounces grated cheese

  1 bunch fresh coriander, chopped

     Pinch of paprika

     Salt and pepper, to taste

F o r   t h e   D o u g h

  1 pound plain flour

1¾ to 2⅓ cups water

F o r   t h e   S o u p

  2 tablespoons olive oil

  1 onion, chopped

  2 tomatoes, skinned and chopped

  1 tablespoon chopped coriander

  1 vegetable stock cube

1¾ cups boiling water

To make the filling, boil and mash the potatoes. Leave to cool. Heat the olive oil in a saucepan and cook the onions for 5 minutes until soft. Add the mushrooms, cover, and cook for 5 minutes or until soft. Leave to cool.

When all the vegetables are cooled, mix with the grated cheese, chopped coriander, salt, and pepper.

To make the dough, mix the flour with enough water to form a smooth dough. Roll out, but not too thinly. Cut into rounds with a 2" pastry cutter. Taking each round, press the edges with your thumb and first two fingers, working around the circle. On one side of the round, place a tablespoonful of the cooled vegetable mixture, then fold over and press the edges together, making sure they are well sealed. Alternatively, hold the round in one hand, and with your thumb and fore-finger gather the edges into a pleat at the top and seal.

Fill a small steamer with water, first boiling the rack so the dumplings do not stick. Bring the water to a boil. Place the momos on the steamer rack, spacing them well apart as they will expand and stick together if they are too close. Steam for 20 minutes, or until they are firm and glossy.

To make the soup, heat the olive oil in a saucepan, add the onion, and cook till soft. Add the tomatoes and chopped coriander and cook for 5 minutes. Dissolve the stock cube in the boiling water and add to the pan. Bring to a boil and sim-mer for 15 minutes. Serve in small bowls as an accompaniment to the dumplings.

Vegetable Curry

Serves 6

½ cup sliced onion

2 tablespoons peanut oil

1 teaspoon freshly grated ginger

2 cloves chopped garlic

½ teaspoon turmeric

½ teaspoon chili powder

½ teaspoon salt

1 cup water

1 pound potatoes, cut into ½" cubes

2 cups cauliflower florets

1 cup chopped tomato

Cayenne pepper to taste

Sauté onions in oil in a large frying pan until golden. Add ginger, garlic, turmeric, chili, and salt and stir for 3 minutes. Add water and potatoes and cook about 15 minutes. Add cauliflower and tomato and cook over low heat till most of the liquid has evaporated and vegetables are tender. Season with cayenne.

A REQUEST FOR RICE

Zen master Ryokan (1758–1831) often wrote of his empty begging bowl. Sometimes his very poem became one.

Bleak, bare, my three-span room;
a wreck, this creaky old body,
now especially in winter months—
I'd have trouble telling you all my ills.
Sipping gruel, I get through the cold night,
counting the days, waiting for sunny spring.
But if I don't ask for a measure of rice,
how can I last out the season?
Pondering, I came up with no workable plan.
so I write this poem, send it to you, old friend.
—translated by Burton Watson

Slow and Sincere

Cooking with sincerity is a trademark of the Zen cook. Martine Batchelor had to learn to adapt and translate both the teachings and the dishes she learned in a Korean monastery, where she trained as a Buddhist nun, to suit her present surroundings and ingredients: an English kitchen and a lay life.

F or ten years I lived as a nun in Zen temples in Korea. Every year I loved to see some food appear just once to mark some very special occasion. For New Year we looked forward to having adzuki bean soup with sticky rice balls for breakfast, five-grain rice at lunch, spicy persimmon punch and sweet rice drink for dessert; for the harvest festival we made half-moon rice cakes filled with sweet bean paste. When the summer was very hot we would be served cold stringy buckwheat noodles in cold soy milk broth (not my favorite, I must say).

Living in a temple, there were ceremonies and celebrations, and on these special days at lunchtime we would get some delicacies like fresh bean curd stew or vegetable pancakes. Vegetable pancakes were one of my favorites. The first ingredient was a batter made with water and flour (no eggs or milk because temple food was traditionally vegan). Then either zucchini or potato slices, or a mixture of finely cut zucchini and potato would be dipped into the batter. This was fried with a little oil in a giant frying cauldron, heated with firewood from the nearby forest. There were also, very occasionally, delicious mung bean pancakes.

Coming back to the West after ten years of very traditional Zen training, I saw that in teaching I had to adapt the practice and the form it took to the sensibilities of the people I met who were interested in Buddhism. In the same way, I realized I could not really cook the Korean temple way due to the lack of ingredients and the resurgence of my French roots. I started to make my own recipes, which combined the two styles of cooking.

Similarly, as Western Buddhists, we cannot avoid understanding the Buddhist teaching through a certain Western framework. We cannot abstract ourselves from the influence of our cultures, milieu, and history. So a certain Western sensitivity will color the way we practice and the way we teach it. However, the practice will still work and have a wonderful taste.

One example of this hybrid cooking style follows.

Zucchini-Almond Pancakes with Eggplant and Tomato Sauce

Serves 4

2 eggs

1¼ cups milk

1 cup ground almonds

1 cup flour

1 small zucchini

Salt and pepper

Herbs, fresh or dried (chopped fine)

1 onion, sliced fine

3 cloves garlic, minced

1 tablespoon olive oil

1 small (10–12 ounce) can tomatoes, pureed, or equivalent fresh tomatoes, chopped

2 large eggplants

Sunflower oil

Paper towels

Mix the eggs and the milk, then add the ground almonds and the flour. Grate the zucchini very fine; add to the mixture. Season with salt and pepper and fresh herbs according to taste. Let rest for 30 minutes.

Meanwhile, fry the onion and garlic in the olive oil over very low heat for 5 minutes. Add the tomatoes and allow to cook for 20 minutes on low heat, uncovered, stirring from time to time.

Cut the eggplant in thin slices (peeled or unpeeled, according to taste). Fry the slices in sunflower oil until soft and allow them to drain on a paper towel. Set aside.

Fry the pancakes (should make 8 pancakes total) in sunflower oil. Serve 2 pancakes per person or layer the pancakes to make a gâteau (layer cake). The idea is to place a pancake on a dish, add some eggplant slices, add some tomato sauce (it should not be too watery), and top it with another pancake or continue to pile pancakes, eggplant, and tomato sauce to make a gâteau, which can then be cut into 4 wedges to serve. This is a dish for a special occasion or when you have a lot of time, as pancakes are time-consuming to cook unless you have many frying pans.

When I was a Zen nun in Korea, a nun told me, "The busier you are, the slower you should go." This has helped me greatly when cooking. When I cook for conferences and suddenly I find myself stressed and pressured, I remember that saying and I go much more slowly and generally discover I am as efficient but much calmer. This saying has also influenced the way I cook. As time passes, I cook simpler food, but I hope it is as delicious. I use fewer ingredients but choose them very carefully for shape, color, and texture. I simplify my cooking so I have more time to do it in peace and with undisturbed awareness. In this way, I devised a dessert that can be quickly made, is versatile in terms of ingredients, and it is a recipe for which I am often asked. It is a mousse but without eggs so you do not have to separate and beat them. It can be a mango or a chocolate mousse, depending on your ingredients and your taste.

Mango Mousse

1 or 2 fresh mangoes or 1 small can mangoes (approx.
   10 ounces)
1 small tub crème fraîche (approx. 6 ounces) and/or 1
   small pot creamy yogurt (approx. 8 ounces)
   Sugar, to taste (optional)
   Vanilla or lemon rind

Purée mango (without juice, if canned) in a blender or food processor, add crème fraîche and/or yogurt, add sugar, vanilla extract or lemon rind (grated fine) to taste. Mix everything by hand, keeping the mixture as light as possible, and serve in individual dishes garnished with a sprig of mint or some delicate cookies.

Chocolate Mousse

 4 ounces chocolate

1¾ ounces butter

 1 small tub crème fraîche (approx. 6 ounces)

 1 small pot of creamy yogurt (approx. 8 ounces)

  Sugar, to taste

  Vanilla (optional)

  Cinnamon (optional)

Melt chocolate with butter in a double boiler over boiling water. When cool, mix with the crème fraîche and the yogurt. Add sugar according to taste. Vanilla extract and cinnamon might add subtle flavorings. Serve in individual dishes with a dollop of crème fraîche and some nice cookies.

A REFLECTION ON MAKING OFFERINGS OF FOOD AND WATER

Buddhist teacher Thubten Chodron reflects on the practice of setting out altar offerings, which can slowly prepare us to give the gift of food—and other gifts—to others with sincerity and true generosity.

Making offerings helps us create positive potential energy and develop our good qualities. At present, we have excessive attachment and miserliness. We tend to keep the biggest and best for ourselves and give the second best or something we don't want to others. But these self-centered attitudes make us always feel poor and dissatisfied, no matter how much we have. We constantly fear losing what little we do have. Such attitudes make us restless and lead us to act dishonestly to get more things or to be unkind to others to protect what we have.

Our purpose in making offerings is to pacify these destructive habits of attachment and miserliness. When making an offering, it's best to do so without any feelings of loss or regret. For this reason, bowls of water are often offered on the shrine. Water is readily accessible so that we can easily habituate ourselves to the thought and action of giving. Thus, we come to feel rich when we give and take pleasure in sharing good things with others.

Thousand-Mile Pie

Monastic eating practices—taking meals together as a group and partaking of the same foods—are aimed at diminishing attachment to the ego. To indulge an individual whim or craving strengthens the sense of separation between self and other, which, from a Buddhist view, increases suffering. Rick Fields tells the story of a monk who abandons the monastic rules for a piece of berry pie.

C hinese Buddhists often spend years on pilgrimage. Heng Ju, a bhikshu [monk] from Gold Mountain [a monastery in the U.S.], took on this practice from San Francisco to Seattle in 1973, bowing the whole way every three steps. Nine months after they began Heng Ju and Heng Yo [his companion] completed on Gold Mountain the thousand-mile pilgrimage. When Heng Ju spoke he recited a verse the master had given him the day of his departure:

> Practicing what is difficult to practice
>   is the conduct of the sage:
> Enduring what is hard to endure is the
>   genuine patience.
> All Buddhas throughout the ten directions
>   have walked down this road.
> The eighty thousand Bodhisattvas have
>   followed right along.
> Blow the magnificent Dharma conch and
>   raise up the cry;
> Shake your precious tin staff, transform
>   stingy greed.
> Your work complete, and result full, a
>   return amidst song of triumph
> Then I'll give my disciple a meal of
>   berry pie!

The story, which everyone [assembled] knew, was that six days after taking the vow to eat only one meal a day [essential to the Theravadin or Southeast Asian tradition of monastic practice], several years prior to his bowing journey, Heng Ju had slipped out of the monastery and eaten a whole batch of pastries. One berry pie was left, and he wrapped it up, put it in his pocket and returned to the monastery. By evening he had begun to think about the pie, and he thought about it all through the abbot's lecture that night. About ten o'clock, when everyone was asleep, he climbed out the bathroom window, onto the fire-escape and up to the roof, where he began to eat.

"But just at that moment [he said] I looked over at the fire escape to see someone else climbing up onto the roof! I stood there terrorstruck, with a mouthful of pie. There was no place I could run. It was the Master! I stood there unmoving for a moment . . . Then I began walking around in a circle on the rooftop as if in deep contemplation. The Master, too, began to circle the roof as if in deep contemplation but he was going in the opposite direction. We passed each other twice without looking at each other, but on the third lap I looked up and saw him grinning like a Cheshire cat. He said four words, 'How does it feel?' That was the famous berry pie incident. The Abbot has been kidding me about it for years now."

When Heng Ju and Heng Yo got back to the monastery after their pilgrimage—they had bowed an extra hundred fifty miles up to the site of a projected monastery, just for good measure—they were welcomed by a dharma assembly: ceremonies, festivities, dharma talks, and a vegetarian feast. Heng Ju ate only one thing, a whole berry pie, presented by the abbott. As he said at the end of his talk that day, "Today you have all had a chance to see a bhikshu who bowed a thousand miles for a piece of pie."

Blackberries with Rose Geranium Leaves

Serves 4

This recipe comes from Greens.

2–3 cups blackberries

6 rose geranium leaves

1–2 tablespoons light brown sugar

Rose geranium blossoms, for garnish

1 cup heavy cream

Sort through the berries and remove any stems and leaves. Rinse the rose geranium leaves and crush them gently in your hands to release their perfume. In a serving dish, make several layers of berries and leaves, with sugar sprinkled lightly over the berries. Cover the bowl and let the berries sit for several hours, or all day, in the refrigerator.

Bring the berries to room temperature before serving; remove the geranium leaves and garnish the berries with the individual pink blossoms. Serve the cream separately in a pitcher.

Huckleberry Pie

Serves 6

Pastry

 1¼ cups all-purpose flour

 1 teaspoon salt

 ⅔ cup vegetable shortening

 ⅓ cup cold water

Filling

 3 cups huckleberries or blueberries, fresh or frozen

 2 tablespoons flour

 ¾ cup sugar

 ⅛ teaspoon salt

 1 tablespoon lemon juice

 1 tablespoon butter

Mix the pastry ingredients with pastry blender, or cut in shortening with 2 knives till mixture is crumbly, each crumb about the size of a pea. Sprinkle water over mixture and blend lightly just till it can be rolled into a ball. Handle as little as possible. Divide in 2, roll out 2 crusts. Line 9" pie pan with 1 crust. Mix berries, flour, sugar, and salt in a bowl, fill crust. Sprinkle lemon juice over the top and dot with butter. Cover with top crust, pricking well. Bake in preheated 425° oven for 45 minutes.

BLESSING

May all beings have happiness
and the causes of happiness
May all beings be free from sorrow
and the causes of sorrow
May all never be separated from
the sacred happiness which is sorrowless
May all live in equanimity,
without attachment or aversion,
believing in the equality of all that lives.
—from the Nyingma Institute, Berkeley, California

Uneaten

Here cookbook author and chef Edward Espe Brown discusses the
practice of preparing food that will remain uneaten.

We have a custom in out meditation tradition which for
many years I found peculiar: offering food to Buddha.
Before breakfast and lunch the cooks make up a small tray of
food, using little dishes with little utensils. In its way it's rather

cute, suggestive of doll house cuisine. Food is put delicately into each wee dish, and then a spoon and chopsticks are set ready to use.

When I was cooking, I found the whole thing rather annoying. Wasn't I busy enough serving food to the community without having to serve food to someone who's not even going to eat it? Whatever was the point? And afterwards, when I collected the uneaten food the Buddha said absolutely nothing about liking this or not liking that, or, "Loved the seasoning on the carrots." No, the Buddha just went on sitting there completely unconcerned.

The first summer I was cooking at Tassajara, Bill (Jakusho) Kwong and his wife Laura came to visit. Jakusho teaches now at the Sonoma Mountain Zen Center. He had been the cook at Zen Center when I first arrived. He and Laura came to help out in the kitchen, and I waited to see how he would handle this bit of ritual. I could not believe how polite and respectful he was while putting food into those tiny bowls: careful, sincere, unhurried, as though serving the most honored of guests. "Please, try this, and perhaps some of this. I'm sure you'll like it." The sweetness of it, serving food which was to be uneaten and unremarked upon.

And, that is the way in which many of these practices work—on a delayed basis. Some twenty-five years later it occurred to me that serving food to Buddha in this fashion was utterly profound: this is the way to cook. Cook the food and serve it. Bow and depart. You've done your part. Make an offering of your food, let go, and walk away.

The following recipe is the creation of Edward Espe Brown.

Winter Squash Soup with Apple, Cumin, and Cardamom

Serves 4 – 6

1½–2 pounds winter squash

1 teaspoon cumin seed

¼ teaspoon cardamom seed

1 yellow onion, sliced

1 tablespoon olive oil

2 cloves garlic, minced

1 tablespoon grated fresh ginger

1 apple, cored and sliced

1 tablespoon lemon juice

Salt

Bake the squash about 1 hour at 375°. Allow it to cool, then cut open, remove seeds, and scoop out the flesh.

Grind the cumin and cardamom in an electric coffee mill used for grinding spices. Sauté the onion in olive oil for 2–3 minutes, then add the garlic, ginger, cumin, and cardamom and continue cooking for another 1–2 minutes.

Add the apple and 3 cups hot water, along with the squash. Cook for 10 minutes or so. When the apple is soft, puree with a hand blender. Season with the lemon juice and salt to taste.

Summer Fruit Soup

Serves 6

3 cups Cabernet Sauvignon
2 pounds assorted red fruits (strawberries, raspberries, pitted cherries, red currants, etc.)
⅔ cup sugar, or to taste
  Whipped cream or crème fraîche

Put the wine into a heavy saucepan and any fruit that needs cooking (cherries). Next dissolve about ⅔ cup sugar in the mixture; let it simmer for about 5 minutes. Remove the pot from the heat and let cool. Add the strawberries and/or raspberries. Pour the mixture into a large serving bowl and refrigerate. Accompany with fresh whipped cream or crème fraîche for a simple, delicious summer dessert. Serve well chilled.

POEM

A poem by ninth-century Chinese poet Layman P'ang, as translated by Burton Watson:

Of a hut in the fields the elder,
I'm the poorest man on earth!
Inside the house there's not one thing:
When I open my mouth it says "empty,
empty."
In the past I had bad friends—
I saved them all, made them priests;
Sitting together in harmony,
I always have them hear of the Mahayana,
At mealtimes carrying bowls for them,
I serve them one and all

Vow

The Jataka or "birth" tales comprise more than 500 legends that recount the lives and compassionate actions of the historical Buddha before he was born as Prince Siddhartha. The stories show that by acting compassionately, any being—crab, hare, or human—can attain buddhahood. Specifically, the parables illustrate the fulfillment of a vow taken by many Buddhists, the Bodhisattva Vow: the promise to liberate all sentient beings. The

*Jataka tale that best embodies both the aspiration and the
application of the selfless Bodhisattva spirit is "The Hungry
Tigress." This version is retold by Andrew Schelling.*

I n a former life, many aeons ago, the Buddha took up residence in a forest hermitage, living the life of a recluse and studying with a resolute mind. Sauntering through the woods one day, admiring the springtime foliage, he rounded a bend near a mountain crevasse and saw a cave. There at the mouth of the cave, but a few feet from him, lay a starving tigress who had just given birth. This tigress was so overcome by her labors, so weak with hunger, that she could scarcely move. The future Buddha noticed her dark and hollowed eyes. He could see each rib distending her hide. Starved and confused, she was turning on her whelps, on her own tiger pups, seeing them only as meat to satisfy her belly. The pups, not comprehending the danger, were sidling up, pawing for her teats.

The Buddha was overcome by horror—for his own well-being he felt no fear, but seeing another sentient being in distress made him tremble and quake like the Himalaya. He thought to himself, "How futile this round of birth and death! Hopeless the world's vanity! Right in front of my eyes hunger forces this creature to transgress the laws of kinship and affection. She is about to feed on her own tiger cubs. I cannot permit this, I must get her some food."

But the next instant he thought, "Why search for meat from some other creature? That can only perpetuate the round of pain and suffering. Here is my own body, meat enough to feed this tigress. Frail, impure, an ungrateful thing—vehicle of suffering—I can make this body a source of nourishment for another! I'd be a fool not to grasp this opportunity. By doing so may I acquire the power to release all creatures from suffering!

And climbing a high ridge, he cast himself down in front of the tigress. On the verge of slaughtering her pups, hearing the sound, she looked across—seeing the fresh corpse, she bounded over and ate it. Thus she and her cubs were saved.

Tempeh in Barbecue Sauce

A *protein-rich recipe for tempeh, cultured soybean cutlets, from Katherine Whitehead, the head cook of Tassajara Zen Practice Center, who was inspired in part by Louise Hagler's recipe for barbecued tofu.*

    6 marinated tempeh squares
    1 medium onion, chopped
  1–2 garlic cloves, minced
  2–3 tablespoons oil
   1⅔ cups canned, diced tomatoes
    ¾ cup water
    ½ cup sugar
    2 tablespoons molasses
    ¼ cup Dijon mustard
    1 teaspoon dried parsley or 2 teaspoons fresh parsley
    ½ teaspoon allspice
    ¼ teaspoon cayenne
    ¼ cup fresh lemon juice

If using commercially marinated tempeh, place tempeh squares in enough boiling water to cover and simmer for 15–20 minutes. If homemade tempeh is used, skip parboiling step and simply add sauce.

In a separate pan, sauté onion and garlic in oil. Add tomatoes, water, sugar, molasses, mustard, parsley, allspice, and cayenne, and simmer for about 1 hour. Then add lemon juice. Arrange tempeh in a lightly oiled 9" x 13" baking pan. Cut each square into 4 strips. Bake at 350° for 30 minutes.

Spinach Egg Drop Soup

Serves 4

A fortifying and warming soup from Kopan Monastery near Katmandu.

2 tablespoons butter

1 tablespoon fresh gingerroot, minced

1 tablespoon fresh garlic, minced

½ cup red onion, diced

¼ cup white flour

4 cups water

1½ cups fresh spinach, chopped

½ cup fresh tomatoes, chopped

½ cup tofu, diced

1 tablespoon soy sauce

½ teaspoon chili powder

1 teaspoon salt

¼ teaspoon ground black pepper

1 egg

Melt butter in a large saucepan over medium heat. Add ginger, garlic, and red onion. Stir-fry over medium heat for 1 minute. Add flour and continue to stir until flour mixture is slightly golden in color, 3–5 minutes. Add water, 1 cup at a time, stirring constantly to prevent lumps from forming. Stir till mixture is smooth. Add spinach, tomatoes, and tofu. Mix well and bring to a boil. Add soy sauce, chili powder, salt, and pepper to taste. Allow to boil 2 more minutes. If soup is too thick, add water. In a small bowl, lightly beat egg. Just before serving, add egg to soup, stirring constantly. Remove from heat and serve hot.

PRAYER

*The following verses are excerpted from Stephen Batchelor's trans-
lation of* A Guide to the Bodhisattva's Way of Life, *composed by
Shantideva in the eighth century.*

May I be the doctor and the medicine
And may I be the nurse
For all sick beings in the world
Until everyone is healed.

May a rain of food and drink descend
To ease the pain of thirst and hunger
And during the aeon of famine
May I change myself into food and drink.

Work

In the Zen tradition, not only were monks expected to beg for alms, they also had to work to grow food. Paul Reps retells this Zen tale.

P ai Chang, the Chinese Zen master of the ninth-century, used to labor with his pupils even at the age of eighty, trimming the gardens, cleaning the grounds, and pruning the trees.

The pupils felt sorry to see the old teacher working so hard, but they knew he would not listen to their advice to stop, so they hid away his tools.

That day the master did not eat. The next day he did not eat, nor the next. "He may be angry because we have hidden his tools," the pupils surmised. "We had better put them back."

The day they did the teacher worked and ate the same as before. In the evening he instructed them, "No work, no food."

Cream of Carrot Soup

Serves 4

  1 pound carrots, chopped

  1 stalk celery, chopped

  1 small turnip, chopped

  1 small onion, chopped

  1 ounce bacon, chopped

  1 ounce butter

1½ pints chicken stock

  1 teaspoon thyme

  1 bay leaf

    Salt and pepper, to taste

 ⅓ cup flour

 ½ pint milk

1–2 teaspoons cream

  1 tablespoon chopped parsley

Sauté vegetables and bacon in butter for 10 minutes without browning. Add stock and seasonings, cover, and simmer gently for 1 hour. Remove bay leaf and mash or blend in blender. Blend flour with milk, add to soup, and bring to boil. Cook gently 2 minutes. Add cream and stir. Add parsley.

The little extra effort required by this recipe is amply repaid.

Kopan Chow Mein

S e r v e s   4

½ cup tofu

Oil for deep frying

1 pound fresh egg noodles

¼ cup vegetable oil

½ tablespoon fresh gingerroot, minced

½ tablespoon garlic, minced

½ cup red onion, diced

1 cup fresh bean sprouts

½ cup fresh or frozen peas

1 cup fresh spinach, chopped

3 cups mixed vegetables, parboiled and chopped

½ teaspoon chili powder (optional)

1–2 tablespoons soy sauce

½ teaspoon salt

¼ teaspoon ground black pepper

Cut tofu into julienne pieces. Heat oil for deep frying in a wok. Add tofu and fry for a few minutes on medium-high heat until golden brown. Remove and drain on paper towels.

In a large saucepan, bring water to a boil. Add noodles. When noddles float to the top, cook 1 to 2 minutes more. Noodles will be cooked again, so do not overcook now. Drain and rinse in cold water. Add 1 teaspoon of oil and toss so they won't stick together. Heat 3 tablespoons oil in wok or skillet over medium heat. Add 1–2 handfuls of noodles. Pan-fry—do

not stir—until slightly crispy, and then flip over. Cook this side till golden brown. Remove and drain on paper towel. Repeat with remaining noodles. Allow 20 minutes for this step. Heat another 2 tablespoons oil in wok or skillet, add ginger, garlic, and red onion. Stir 1 minute. Add bean sprouts; mix well another minute. Add peas and spinach; continue to stir-fry another minute. Then add the mixed vegetables and fried tofu. Stir-fry 1–2 minutes more. Add pan-fried noodles and mix well. Add seasonings to taste and continue to stir 1 minute more. Remove from heat and serve hot.

POEM

This poem was written by Nyogen Senzaki, the first Zen master to reside in the United States.

Is your hunger satisfied when another eats?
Is your thirst quenched when another drinks?
Are you rested when another sleeps?
By whose efforts will you be enlightened?
—translated by Nyogen Senzaki and Ruth McCandless

Xuefeng

A famous tenzo, or head cook, mentioned in Dogen's
"Instructions to the Cook" and many other Zen texts, Xuefeng
[also translated as Hsueh Feng] showed his realization—his
freedom from dualistic thinking—by overturning a pot. This
passage is excerpted from The Blue Cliff Record, a collection of
koans and commentary, translated by Thomas Cleary and J. C.
Cleary.

H sueh Feng [Xuefeng], teaching his assembly, said, "Pick up the whole great Earth in your fingers, and it's as big as a grain of rice." There was something extraordinary in the way this ancient guided people and benefited beings. He was indefatigably rigorous; three times he climbed Mount T'ou Tzu, nine times he went to Tung Shan. Wherever he went, he would set up his lacquer tub and wooden spoon and serve as the rice steward, just for the sake of penetrating this matter.

When he arrived at Tung Shan, he served as rice steward: one day, Tung Shan asked Hsueh Feng [Xuefeng], "What are you doing?" Hsueh Feng [Xuefeng] said, "Cleaning rice." Tung Shan asked, "Are you washing the grit to get rid of the rice, or are you washing the rice to get rid of the grit?" Hsueh Feng said, "Grit and rice are both removed at once." Tung Shan said, "What will everybody eat?" Hsueh Feng then overturned the basin.

An excerpt from Uchiyama Roshi's commentary on the same story:

There is no human life in which there is no difference drawn between miso [soybean paste] and *kuso* [excrement]. This is why the question arises in the *Tenzo Kyokun* [Dogen's *Instructions to the Cook*] about whether one separates the sand from the rice or the rice from the sand. Apparently in olden days in China, the rice polishing process was not very efficient, and there were a lot of tiny pebbles mixed in with the rice. The first thing the tenzo had to do was pick the tiny stones out of the rice before it was cooked. In this respect there can be no doubt that food fit for human consumption lies at the point where we have to discriminate, but what we must not forget is the fundamental attitude grounding this discrimination: everything we encounter is our life. This is the attitude of Big Mind.

Practically speaking, just how does this work? Earlier, I quoted a passage from the *Tenzo Kyokun* regarding Big Mind:

"Magnanimous Mind is like a mountain, stable and impartial. Exemplifying the ocean, it is tolerant and views everything from the broadest perspective. Having a Magnanimous Mind means being without prejudice and refusing to take sides. When carrying something that weighs an ounce, do not think of it as light, and likewise, when you have to carry fifty pounds, do not think of it as heavy. Do not get carried away by the sounds of spring, nor become heavy-hearted upon seeing the colors of fall. View the changes of the seasons as a whole, and weigh the relativeness of light and heavy from a broad perspective. It is then you should write, understand, and study the character for magnanimous."

Usually, pound and ounce are thought of as units of weight. This metaphor means, however, that you should not be swayed by the values of society nor get all excited simply because it is spring—finding yourself in favorable circumstances, adversity, despair, and exaltation all as the scenery of your life. This is what lies behind the expression *Big Mind*.

Dal

1 cup dry lentils, black or yellow

⅛ cup vegetable oil

½ cup red onion, diced

1 tablespoon fresh gingerroot, minced

1 tablespoon fresh garlic, minced

1 teaspoon turmeric

1 teaspoon chili powder

1 teaspoon Kopan Masala (see next page)

4 cups water

1 teaspoon salt

¼ cup green onion, chopped

2 tablespoons Chinese parsley (cilantro), chopped

Rinse lentils 2 or 3 times with cool water. Cover with water and set aside for 1 hour. Heat oil in a large saucepan over medium heat. Add red onion, ginger, garlic, turmeric, chili powder, and masala. Stir-fry over medium to medium-high heat for 1 minute. Drain and add lentils and continue to stir-fry for 2–3 minutes. Add water and bring to a boil. Allow to simmer over low to medium-low heat for 30 minutes or until lentils are soft. Add more water if dal becomes too thick. Salt to taste. Just before serving, add green onion and Chinese parsley. Mix well. Serve hot.

Kopan Masala

Makes ¹/₂ cup

⅓ cup coriander seeds

¼ cup cumin

10 black cardamom pods, peeled

15 pale green cardamom pods, peeled

25 cloves

2 cinnamon sticks, broken up

1 teaspoon black peppercorns

¼ teaspoon fresh nutmeg, ground

Mix together and grind finely, but not to powder, with a mortar and pestle, rolling pin, coffee grinder, or a food processor. Store in airtight jar.

Tibetan Barley Soup

Serves 2 – 4

A *recipe from the Zen fellowship:*

Barley can thrive even on marginal land. Like the Zen practitioner, it is at home everywhere. You can get pot barley at health food stores. If possible avoid the pearled, or polished barley, which is less tasty and less nutritious.

Cut up enough mushrooms to measure 2 cups. Melt 2 table-spoons butter, (yak butter if available) in a large saucepan and stir in vegetables until they are well coated. Continue cooking over medium heat until softened, stirring occasionally. Mix in ¼ cup pot barley and then add 4 cups water (preferably from the nearest mountain spring). Bring rapidly to a boil, then sim-mer about an hour, covered. Just before it is done, add 1 table-spoon *shoyu* (soy sauce) and a grind or so of pepper, if desired. When the soup is ready, it should be of a chowder-like thick-ness and the grains should be soft but chewy. There will be a golden sheen on the surface and the heavenly smell will waft you across the Himalayas.

A REFLECTION

Where there is alot of fuss about "spirituality," "enlightenment" or just "turning on," it is often because there are buzzards hovering around a corpse. This hovering, this circling, this descending, this celebration of victory, are not what is meant by the Study of Zen—even though they may be a highly useful exercise in other contexts. And they enrich the birds of appetite.

Zen enriches no one. There is no body to be found. The birds may come and circle for a while in the place where it is thought to be. But they soon go elsewhere. When they are gone, the "nothing," the "no-body" that was there, suddenly appears. That is Zen. It was there all the time but the scavengers missed it, because it was not their kind of prey.
—Thomas Merton, from <u>Zen and the Birds of Appetite</u>

Yogi

This Tibetan tale is retold by Buddhist scholar Miranda Shaw.

L uipa received his decisive lesson in the form of an insult
from a woman. Luipa, a yogi of princely birth, had been
practicing Tantric meditation for many years and considered
himself to be above reproach when he ran into a yogini tavern
owner. With her clairvoyant vision, she perceived a small but

obdurate knot of royal pride in his heart, despite his many years of renunciation. Instead of giving him something from the menu, she served him a bowl of moldy leftovers. Luipa threw the bowl into the street in disgust and shouted, "How dare you serve garbage to a yogi?" She shot back, "How can an epicure attain enlightenment?" Stung by the accuracy of her riposte, he saw where to direct his efforts in order to scale the final peak of enlightenment. He took up residence on a river-bank and began to live on fish entrails discarded by the fisher-men. Through this practice, Luipa attained a state of continual bliss in which the fish entrails tasted just like ambrosial nectar.

Fish Chowder

Serves 6

4 onions, chopped

2 cloves garlic, chopped fine

½ cup olive oil

1 quart tomatoes

1 green pepper, thinly sliced

2 fish heads

2 cups white wine

2 tiny hot peppers, diced fine

2 bay leaves

1 teaspoon thyme

Salt and pepper to taste

2 pounds firm white fish, cut into chunks

1 pound prawns

1 pound crabmeat

Mussels or clams (optional)

2 cups fresh peas

Sauté onions and garlic in oil until translucent. Add tomatoes and green pepper; simmer for 30 minutes. Add fish heads and wine and simmer 20 minutes. Remove fish heads and discard; puree the rest of the mixture. Add hot pepper and other seasonings. (May hold at this point.) Add fish cut into chunks, prawns, crabmeat, and shellfish, if using.

Cook 5 minutes. Add peas. Cook until done. Season to taste.

This poem is one of the Theragatha *or songs composed by the personal disciples of the Buddha. The translation was done by Andrew Schelling.*

I came down from my
mountain hut
into the streets one day
to beg food

I stopped where a leper
was feeding himself
With his rotted leper's hand
into my bowl
he threw a scrap

into my bowl as he
threw it
one of his fingers broke and also fell
I simply leaned against a wall
and ate

Taking whatever scraps
are tossed
finding medicine
in cow-dung

sleeping
beneath a tree and wrapped in
tattered robes—
only a man like that
walks free in all the four
directions

only a man like that
walks free

Zazen

Zazen is Zen sitting meditation. In a commentary on Dogen's
"Instructions to the Cook," or "Tenzo Kyokun," Zen master
Kosho Uchiyama Roshi claims that cooking as practice is nothing
other than taking zazen into the kitchen, into one's daily life. He
goes on to say that the spiritual life and practical, everyday life are
one and the same; the wholehearted practice of sitting and the
wholehearted practice of cooking are themselves enlightenment.

Whatever goal we grab onto, accumulating money or credentials, gaining status, or having a family, can decline and fall apart. That way of life has no true stability. There is an interesting expression in Japanese that captures the sense of this: "One's goal and the Etchu fundoshi (loincloth) both part in front." When doing zazen we practice ceasing to project some goal separate from the Self. Instead, we learn to live out completely that Self that settles upon itself. This is why Dogen Zenji writes that zazen is the standard or model of true peace and tranquillity.

Certain problems arise concerning this Self that employs zazen as a standard. When I use the term Self, I am not referring to some fixed entity; the Self is life, and life is functioning. Functioning means activity which works toward the world in which the Self lives. When I talk of a "Self settling upon itself," do not interpret this to mean a withdrawing and escaping from society. On the contrary, this expression means that your life manifests itself as life. It is a Self that works to settle or bring composure to everything you encounter in your life.

Without being dependent upon anything, and being willing to accept and face whatever comes up—this is the attitude of magnanimity, or in Japanese, daishin [Big Mind]. Next, functioning with the attitude of a parent, seeing all the people and events we encounter in our lives as our children—this is Parental mind.

Taking the discussion one step further, discovering the true meaning of our lives through this parental attitude is called kishin, or Joyful Mind. In the Tenzo Kyokun, Big Mind, Parental Mind, and Joyful Mind are called the "three minds."

The teaching of the Tenzo Kyokun is, through our practice of preparing meals, to develop these attitudes in order that they become integrated into the way we live out all the aspects of our lives.

"When you prepare food, do not see with ordinary eyes and do not think with ordinary mind. Take up a blade of grass and construct a treasure king's land; enter into a particle of dust and turn the great dharma wheel. Do not arouse disdainful mind when you prepare a broth of wild grasses; do not arouse joyful mind when you prepare a fine cream soup. Where there is no discrimination, how can there be distaste?"
—Dogen Zenji, as translated by Kazuaki Tanahashi and Arnold Kotler

EVERYTHING IS BEST

When Banzan was walking through a market he overheard a conversation between a butcher and his customer.
"Give me the best piece of meat you have," said the customer.
"Everything in my shop is the best," replied the butcher.
"You cannot find here any piece of meat that is not the best."
At these words Banzan became enlightened.
—Paul Reps

Acknowledgments

Thanks to all who graciously offered treasured recipes, stories, and meal blessings for inclusion in this book. In addition, to all those acknowledged below, I'd like to express my gratitude to Sean McCloud, Christine S. Tonkinson, and Barry Langford.

Introduction

Excerpt from *Zen Flesh, Zen Bones* by Paul Reps. Reprinted by permission of Charles E. Tuttle Co., Inc., of Tokyo, Japan.

Awake

Excerpt from *A Life of the Buddha* by Michael Edwardes. Courtesy Michael Edwardes and The Folio Society.

A Simple Rice Pudding courtesy the editors of *Tricycle: The Buddhist Review.*

Asparagus Risotto courtesy the editors of *Tricycle: The Buddhist Review.*

Beancurd and Fried Rice from *The Penniless Vegetarian* by David Scott, Rider Books (UK), ISBN 0-7126-5261-2. Permission granted by the author.

Tomato and Rice Soup courtesy the editors of *Tricycle: The Buddhist Review.*

Original haiku by Sallie Tisdale. Permission granted by the author.

Buddha

Excerpt from *Zen Mind, Beginner's Mind* by Shunryu Suzuki Roshi. Reprinted by permission of Weatherhill.

Focaccia courtesy the editors of *Tricycle: The Buddhist Review*.

Puja Bread from *The Kopan Cookbook: Vegetarian Recipes from a Tibetan Monastery*, by Betty Jung, © 1992, published by Chronicle Books, San Francisco.

Gingerbread courtesy the editors of *Tricycle: The Buddhist Review*.

Challah courtesy the editors of *Tricycle: The Buddhist Review*.

From *The Wisdom of No Escape* by Pema Chodron. Published by Shambhala Publications, Inc., 300 Massachusetts Avenue, Boston, MA 02115.

Changes

Excerpt and recipes from *Food for Solitude* by Francine Schiff. Published by Element Books of Rockport, Massachusetts and Shaftesbury, Dorset, England. Reprinted by kind permission of the Publisher.

A Retreat Tortilla recipe by Michael Roach. Permission granted by the author.

Funny Stuff recipe by James Thornton. Permission granted by the author.

Blessing by Ayya Khema. Permission granted by the author.

Dharma

Excerpts from *The Metaphysics of Cooking* and *The Metaphysics of Eating* by John Daido Loori. Reprinted by permission of Dharma Communications.

Free-Range Coq au Vin courtesy the editors of *Tricycle: The Buddhist Review*.

"Guidelines for Mindful Eating" and Lentil Soup recipe by Christina Feldman. Permission granted by the author.

"One Should Not Talk to a Skilled Hunter about What is Forbidden by the Buddha," from *Turtle Island*. Copyright © 1974 by Gary Snyder. Reprinted by permission of New Directions Publishing Corp., and Gary Snyder.

Ego

Excerpt and recipes by Pat Enkyo O'Hara. Permission granted by the author.

Apple Crisp courtesy the editors of *Tricycle: The Buddhist Review*.

Haiku from *On Love and Barley: Haiku of Basho*, translated by Lucien Stryk. Copyright © 1985 by Lucien Stryk. Published by Penguin Books Ltd.

Feast

Essay and blessing by Lama Surya Das. Permission granted by the author.

Sukiyaki courtesy the editors of *Tricycle: The Buddhist Review*.

Tibetan Butter Tea recipe by Marilyn Stablein.

Grace

"Grace" from *The Practice of the Wild* by Gary Snyder. Copyright © 1990 by Gary Snyder. Reprinted by permission of North Point Press, a division of Farrar, Straus & Giroux, Inc., and the author.

Canned Corn by Laura Carter Holloway Langford.

Grammy's Butter Cookies by Carole Tonkinson.

Indian Pudding courtesy the editors of *Tricycle: The Buddhist Review*.

From *Ryokan: Zen Monk-Poet of Japan* translated by Burton Watson. Copyright © 1977 by Columbia University Press. Reprinted with permission of the publisher.

Hungry Ghost

Essay by Mark Epstein. Permission granted by the author.

Light Vinegared Eggplant from *The Heart of Zen Cuisine* by Soei Yoneda published by Kodansha International Ltd. Copyright © 1982 by Kodansha International Ltd. Reprinted by permission. All rights reserved.

Vegetarian Chilli courtesy the editors of *Tricycle: The Buddhist Review*.

Verse of the Saba from *The Training of the Zen Monk* by D. T. Suzuki. Published by Simon & Schuster.

Innocence

Essay by John McClellan. Permission granted by the author.

"How to Make Stew in the Pinacate Desert" by Gary Snyder, from *The Back Country*. Copyright © 1968 by Gary Snyder. Reprinted by permission of New Directions Publishing Corp. and Gary Snyder.

Red Cooked Beancurd and Cucumber from *The Penniless Vegetarian* by David Scott, Rider Books (UK), ISBN 0-7126-5261-2. Permission granted by the author.

Steak Fajitas courtesy the editors of *Tricycle: The Buddhist Review*.

"Grace Before Meat" is from the volume *Heavy Breathing* published by Four Seasons Foundation, San Francisco, 1983. Copyright © 1983 by Philip Whalen and reprinted here with his permission.

Joshu's Bowls

From *Gateless Gate*, translated with commentary by Koun Yamada Roshi. Copyright © 1990 by the Estate of Koun Yamada Roshi. Published by the University of Arizona Press.

"A Recipe for Cleaning the Mind" excerpted from *Instructions to the Cook: A Zen Master's Lessons in Living a Life that Matters* by Bernard Glassman and Rick Fields. Copyright © 1996 by the Zen Community of New York. Published by Bell Tower, member of the Crown Publishing Group. Reprinted by permission of the publisher.

Apple Soufflé courtesy the editors of *Tricycle: The Buddhist Review*.

Floating Islands courtesy the editors of *Tricycle: The Buddhist Review*.

Haiku from *On Love and Barley: Haiku of Basho,* translated by Lucien Stryk. Copyright © 1985 by Lucien Stryk. Published by Penguin Books Ltd.

Karmapa

Essay by Helen Tworkov. Permission granted by the author.

Recipes courtesy the editors of *Tricycle: The Buddhist Review*.

Blessing by Shakyamuni Buddha from *Thus Have I Heard: The Long Discourses of the Buddha,* translated from the *Pali Canon* by Maurice Walshe. Published by Wisdom Publications, 361 Newbury Street, Boston, MA, USA.

Last Meal

Essay by Stuart Smithers. Permission granted by the author.

From *Persephone's Quest,* by Gordon Wasson. Copyright © 1988 by Yale University Press. Reprinted with permission of the publisher.

Cashew Rice from *The Kopan Cookbook: Vegetarian Recipes from a Tibetan Monastery,* by Betty Jung, © 1992, published by Chronicle Books, San Francisco.

Hearty Stew with Seasoned Dumplings courtesy the editors of *Tricycle: The Buddhist Review*.

"[I Burn up the Deer in My Body]" from *Ring of Bone* by Lew Welch, copyright © 1973 by Grey Fox Press. Reprinted by permission of Grey Fox Press.

Middle Way

Excerpts from *From the Zen Kitchen to Enlightenment: Refining Your Life* by Zen master Dogen and Kosho Uchiyama, Weatherhill. Reprinted by permission of the publisher.

Swiss Muesli courtesy the editors of *Tricycle: The Buddhist Review*.

Green Pea Soup with Mint courtesy the editors of *Tricycle: The Buddhist Review*.

Blessing by Michael Roach. Permission granted by the author.

Nature

Excerpts and recipes from *The Heart of Zen Cuisine* by Soei Yoneda published by Kodansha International Ltd. Copyright © 1982 by Kodansha International Ltd. Reprinted by permission. All rights reserved.

Blessing reprinted from *Present Moment Wonderful Moment: Mindfulness Verses for Everyday Living* by Thich Nhat Hanh (1990) with permission of Parallax Press, Berkeley, California.

Oryoki

Excerpts and meal *gatha* from a compilation of Maezumi Roshi's teachings. Permission granted by Wendy Egyoku Nakao.

Savory Cornbread recipe by Ed Rothfarb. Permission granted by the author.

Black Bean and Roasted Pepper Salad courtesy the editors of *Tricycle: The Buddhist Review*.

Preparation

"Instructions to the Tenzo," translated by Arnold Kotler and Kazuaki Tanahashi, from *Moon in a Dewdrop: Writings of Zen master Dogen*, edited by Kazuaki Tanahashi. Copyright © 1985 by the San Francisco Zen Center. Reprinted by permission of North Point Press, a division of Farrar, Straus & Giroux, Inc.

Citrus Salad with Bitter Greens from *Fields of Greens* by Annie Sommerville. Copyright © 1993 by Annie Sommerville. Used by permission of Bantam Books, a division of Bantam Doubleday Dell Publishing Group, Inc.

Beet Salad with Watercress from *Tassajara Cooking* by Edward Espe Brown; copyright © 1985. Reprinted by arrangement with Shambhala Publications, Inc., 300 Massachusetts Avenue, Boston, MA 02115.

"Making Salad" by Margaret Gibson from *Out in the Open*, 1989, Louisiana State University Press. Reprinted by permission of the author.

Qualities

Excerpts by Lama Yeshe reprinted from *The Tantric Path of Purification* with permission of Wisdom Publications, 361 Newbury Street, Boston, MA, USA.

Nectarine Chutney courtesy the editors of *Tricycle: The Buddhist Review*.

Chicken Breasts with Nectarines courtesy the editors of *Tricyle: the Buddhist Review*.

From *Ryokan: Zen Monk-Poet of Japan* translated by Burton Watson. Copyright © 1977 by Columbia University Press. Reprinted with permission of the publisher.

Receiving

Excerpts from *Zen Inklings* by Donald Richie. Copyright © 1994, Weatherhill. Reprinted with permission of the publisher.

The Dalai Lama's Momos from *Recipes for Peace*. Published 1995 by Vermilion (UK).

Vegetable Curry courtesy the editors of *Tricycle: The Buddhist Review*.

From *Ryokan: Zen Monk-Poet of Japan* translated by Burton Watson. Copyright © 1977 by Columbia University Press. Reprinted with permission of the publisher.

India Book: Essays and Translations from Indian Asia, O
Books, 1993. Permission granted by the author.

Tempeh in Barbecue Sauce by Katie Whitehead. Permission
granted by the author.

Spinach Egg Drop Soup from *The Kopan Cookbook:
Vegetarian Recipes from a Tibetan Monastery,* by Betty
Jung, © 1992, published by Chronicle Books, San
Francisco.

Prayer from *A Guide to the Bodhisattva's Way of Life* by
Shantideva, translated by Stephen Batchelor.
Reprinted by permission of the Library of Tibetan
Works and Archives, Dharamsala.

Work

Zen tale from *Zen Flesh, Zen Bones* by Paul Reps. Reprinted
by permission of Charles E. Tuttle Co., Inc., of Tokyo,
Japan.

Cream of Carrot Soup courtesy the editors of *Tricycle: The
Buddhist Review.*

Kopan Chow Mein from *The Kopan Cookbook: Vegetarian
Recipes from a Tibetan Monastery,* by Betty Jung, ©
1992, published by Chronicle Books, San Francisco.

Excerpt from *Buddhism and Zen* by Nyogen Senzaki and Ruth
McCandless. Permission granted by Duncan S.
McCandless.

Xuefeng

Story of Xuefeng from *The Blue Cliff Record* translated by
Thomas Cleary and J. C. Cleary, copyright © 1977.
Reprinted by arrangement with Shambhala Publications,
Inc., 300 Massachusetts Avenue, Boston, MA 02115.

Commentary from *From the Zen Kitchen to Enlightenment:
Refining Your Life* by Zen master Dogen and Kosho
Uchiyama, Weatherhill. Reprinted by permission of
the publisher.

Dal recipe from *The Kopan Cookbook: Vegetarian Recipes from a Tibetan Monastery*, by Betty Jung, © 1992, published by Chronicle Books, San Francisco.

Kopan Masala from *The Kopan Cookbook: Vegetarian Recipes from a Tibetan Monastery*, by Betty Jung, © 1992, published by Chronicle Books, San Francisco.

Tibetan Barley Soup courtesy Zen Fellowship, British Columbia, Canada.

Excerpt by Thomas Merton, from *Zen and the Birds of Appetite*. Published by New Directions Publishing Corp.

Yogi

A Tibetan tale from *Passionate Enlightenment: Women in Tantric Buddhism* by Miranda Shaw, copyright © 1994, Princeton University Press. Reprinted by permission of the publisher.

Fish Chowder courtesy the editors of *Tricycle: The Buddhist Review*.

"Kasapa the Great," copyright © 1994 by Andrew Schelling. From *The Quenching of the Lamp*, Rodent Press, 1994.

Zazen

Excerpt from *From the Zen Kitchen to Enlightenment: Refining Your Life* by Zen master Dogen and Kosho Uchiyama, Weatherhill. Reprinted by permission of the publisher.

"Instructions to the Tenzo," translated by Arnold Kotler and Kazuaki Tanahashi, from *Moon in a Dewdrop: Writings of Zen master Dogen*, edited by Kazuaki Tanahashi. Copyright © 1985 by the San Francisco Zen Center. Reprinted by permission of North Point Press, a division of Farrar, Straus & Giroux, Inc.

Excerpt from *Zen Flesh, Zen Bones* by Paul Reps. Reprinted by permission of Charles E. Tuttle Co., Inc., of Tokyo, Japan.